"I have so enjoyed reading Tim Keesee's books. He is truly a 'frontlines' brother in Christ who tells it like it is on the battlefield / mission field."

**Joni Eareckson Tada,** Founder and CEO, Joni and Friends; author, *Joni* and *A Place of Healing*

"Tim Keesee is both a master storyteller and faithful theologian. Each page is a poetic narrative of faith, hardship, and Jesus building his world through weak and ordinary people. *A Company of Heroes* pulses with the resolute energy of God's saving love. Keesee writes, 'In the name of Jesus, demons are cast out—and in the name of Jesus, fear is cast out.' That God himself saves you from the fear of man just might be the most misunderstood reality of the modern church. The love of Christ and the perseverance of the saints together will subdue forces of evil and change the course of history. This book represents a poetic collaboration of Keesee and a modern-day great cloud of witnesses, and each chapter displays the highest achievement of missionary valor. All Christians should read this book."

**Rosaria Butterfield,** Former Professor of English, Syracuse University; author, *The Gospel Comes with a House Key*

"Tim Keesee's journals bring to light stories of mercy, endurance, and audacity. The heroes in this book are the hands and feet of Jesus—hands scarred and stained by service and feet that go to hard places with the gospel message that shatters darkness and sets captives free."

**Jim DeMint,** former United States senator; Chairman, Conservative Partnership Institute

"One of the greatest joys of being a pastor is hearing people tell me their stories of God's grace in their lives. *A Company of Heroes* is a book of stories of the amazing grace of God and the power of the Holy Spirit in the lives of faithful servants of the gospel of Jesus Christ. Their stories help us to know we're not alone, and they help us to remember that our lives and our stories are not worthless or meaningless if we are living for God's glory and not our own."

**Burk Parsons,** Senior Pastor, Saint Andrew's Chapel, Sanford, Florida; Editor, *Tabletalk*

"Peopling that great heavenly choir is among the missionary's greatest motivations. Tim Keesee compels us to sit at the feet of this great cloud of witnesses by presenting a kaleidoscope of missionary lives. From mosques to Mormons—from first world to third—he urges us to lock shields with the great soldiers and choristers of the past and present. In *A Company of Heroes*, Keesee writes brilliantly as a reporter and lover of gospel advance."

**Paul Schlehlein,** missionary church planter, South Africa; author, *John G. Paton: Missionary to the Cannibals of the South Seas*

A Company of Heroes

# A Company of Heroes

Portraits from the Gospel's Global Advance

Tim Keesee

**CROSSWAY**®

WHEATON, ILLINOIS

## Library of Congress Cataloging-in-Publication Data

Names: Keesee, Timothy.
Title: A company of heroes : portraits from the gospel's global advance / Tim Keesee.
Description: Wheaton, Illinois : Crossway, 2019. | Includes bibliographical references.
Identifiers: LCCN 2018026390 (print) | LCCN 2018043262 (ebook) | ISBN 9781433562587 (pdf)
    | ISBN 9781433562594 (mobi) | ISBN 9781433562600 (epub) | ISBN 9781433562570 (trade
    paperback) | ISBN 9781433562600 (epub) | ISBN 9781433562594 (mobipocket)
Subjects: LCSH: Christian biography.
Classification: LCC BR1700.3 (ebook) | LCC BR1700.3 .C67 2019 (print) | DDC 270.092/2—dc23
LC record available at https://lccn.loc.gov/2018026390

To Debbie,
in the company of heroes

# Contents

# Foreword

I write these words at the end of a year-long journey around the world. Twelve times in the past year I boarded a plane and began a long journey to a distant nation. Twelve times I disembarked and got oriented and began a search—a search for objects related to the long and storied history of the Christian church. I scoured colleges and cathedrals, libraries and museums, always on the lookout for objects that would tell a story beyond themselves. I found some incredible artifacts. In the National Archives of Northern Ireland I found the Bible that Amy Carmichael had pored over for so many years as a bedridden invalid in southern India. In a little museum in England I found the snuffbox Andrew Fuller had pulled from his pocket and passed around the room as a makeshift collection basket upon the founding of the Baptist Missionary Society. In a new exhibit in China I found Hudson Taylor's gravestone which for so many years had been lost—discarded and covered over by the Communist government. I found all these and so many more. It was an inspiring year.

Yet over the course of the year it slowly dawned on me that I was discovering an even better, ever more precious treasure. Everywhere I went, I met Christians. I landed in a major city in China and was immediately welcomed for a meal by the pastor of an underground church. I landed in Australia and was invited to stay with some newlyweds who had prepared a spare bedroom specially for me. I flew over to Auckland, New Zealand, and was invited to stay as long as I wanted in the home of some believers there. In England and India and South Korea brothers and sisters in the Lord gladly gave up their time to drive me many miles and to provide personalized tours. I joined into formal or informal worship services in Brazil, Ecuador, Israel, the Philippines, South Africa, Zambia, and elsewhere.

I came to learn that even though those treasures of church history are inspiring and worth seeing, the greatest treasures can't be found behind glass in museums. The most valuable artifacts of the history of the Christian faith aren't neatly labeled in library stacks. The most enduring relics aren't boxed up in dusty basement archives. Those objects are wonderful and inspiring and worth pursuing around the world. But the true treasure is found in those posh edifices and ramshackle huts we call churches. The greatest treasure is God's redeemed people.

For years now, my friend Tim Keesee has been scouring the world for that kind of treasure. His search has led him to pastors in the world's most dangerous nations, to missionaries who have left behind family and comfort to take the gospel to distant lands, and to people in his own hometown who have labored silently but faithfully. Much of his search is documented in his incredible *Dispatches from the Front* series of videos that I've watched and recommended countless times. More recently I've been thrilled to see him also document it in books like this one. With one eye on the present and one on the past, he powerfully tells the stories of dedicated men and women from today and days gone by. I encourage you to join him on this journey and to come to see and know the greatest treasures in the world.

Tim Challies

# Acknowledgments

Recently an intrepid missionary friend wrote to me words that capture my own heart: "There are few things I enjoy more than meeting and interacting with other brothers and sisters in Christ. As I get older, the pool in which these saints reside gets deeper and wider. The joy increases too."

To the saints in this book, our fellowship in the gospel is indeed deep and wide because it flows from the saving grace of Jesus that is deeper, wider, and sweeter still. This fellowship is a taste of heaven. I am truly blessed to be the reporter and am grateful to the men and women in this book—my friends, my heroes—who trusted me to tell their stories despite the risks they face as they live on mission in hard places.

I am thankful for so many who made this book a reality. For the remarkable team at Frontline Missions International—the men and women on the field as well as those on the home front. You shouldered even more of the work while I was working on this project—as always, I am grateful for you.

For my Epaphras-like friend, Steve Leatherwood, who is a beloved coworker (Col. 1:7). For John Hutcheson, Ben Ebner, Allan Sherer, Andy Johnson, Pete Hansen, and Brannon McAllister with whom I have shared many of the miles and muddy roads that run through the pages of this book.

Many encouragers came alongside me, literally and figuratively, as I traveled and wrote, by offering a timely word, good coffee, or a walk in the woods. I think especially of Gloria Furman (for all the "book scheming" we did together in shaping this book); Kevin and Leslie Cathey (you are gifts of grace and strength to me); Julie Zickefoose (my inimitable friend and fellow writer); Rosaria Butterfield (my faithful prayer partner in this venture—you always had my back); my pastor Trent Hunter (thank you for your genuine interest and cheer and for your Barnabas-like encouragement over the past year of writing and traveling); Chun Lai at Westminster Seminary (an unsung hero of the *Dispatches from the Front* films and a wise counselor as I wrote this book); and Jonathan Henning (like your namesake in the Bible, you are a strong and faithful friend who in your dark hour reminded me to look up and know "you, O LORD, are a shield about me, my glory, and the lifter of my head" [Ps. 3:3]).

As usual, the Crossway team was superb. I am particularly grateful to Justin Taylor for his friendship and guidance and to Tara Davis, my über-editor once again, as well as to Nick Chiodras who did the excellent maps that open each chapter. Thank you for getting this book over the finish line!

Finally, to my family: I'm grateful to my daughter, Sarah, and son, Tim—both gifted wordsmiths—for the helpful suggestions they provided throughout the book. You both continue to make your father's heart glad. Debbie, you have a share in every page that follows. By love and prayer you time and time again have sent me on my "journey in a manner worthy of God" (3 John 6). You are numbered among the company of heroes.

# Introduction

"Grandpa, were you a hero in the war?" The old man had parachuted behind enemy lines during the D-Day invasion forty years earlier. He was part of a crack team that, against superior numbers and weaponry, took out an entire German artillery battery—and thus spared the lives of hundreds of Americans landing on the beachhead at Utah. He was awarded the Bronze Star for valor that day, and after Normandy, he went on to fight with distinction. But looking beyond the memories and medals and into the eyes of his grandson, he answered simply and sincerely, "No, but I served in a company of heroes."[1]

Across the world, I've walked point with a company of heroes, too. We've shared jungle paths, desert roads, and city streets on five continents. These brothers and sisters are foot soldiers in the long campaign as Christ builds his church across the centuries and among all peoples. Their stories are drawn from my journals—often written in motion as they went about their days. Viewers of the *Dispatches from the Front* film series may recognize some of them, although here I can share their lives more fully without the restraints of filming and security. Other heroes whose stories I tell serve in hard and hard-to-reach places. Their actual names can't be written here, but they are written in heaven. As Paul described, they are "unknown, and yet well known" (2 Cor. 6:9) because they labor in obscurity, but God is with them.

I also want to introduce you to heroes of the past. Over the years, yellowing books, obscure footnotes, and neglected tombstones have set me out on serendipitous detours to flesh out the lives of gospel pioneers whose courage, faith, and vision shook iron gates and broke deep darkness. Others would follow and build a road over the trail left by the first missionaries—paths sometimes marked by their untimely graves. Some of these intrepid saints are famous and quotable—others were known to only a small circle of rope-holders and left no memoirs or monuments. Whether well-known or unknown, past or present, their stories are important reminders that the gospel does not only reach across the globe, but it also spans generations and centuries. This is why I love to spend time with missionaries on the field and then go and brush off the tracks left in the region by pioneers of a century past. It's a kind of gospel archaeology that reminds me of God's faithfulness as "one generation shall commend your works to another, and shall declare your mighty acts" (Ps. 145:4).

## Joy and Perspective

Many years ago I was in Albania at a time when the little Balkan country was emerging from nearly fifty years under a brutal, Communist dictatorship. Among the Iron Curtain countries, Albania was considered the "North Korea" of Eastern Europe because of the isolation, deprivation, and persecution that the people suffered for decades. When Communism collapsed in 1990, there was no known church in the entire country, but God showed his great mercy to the people of Albania as the gospel was preached to even the most remote corners of the country so that within twenty years, there were Albanian congregations in every city and in most towns throughout the nation![2]

During those first years of freedom and gospel advance, a missionary friend invited me to teach a short series on church history to his little congregation of first-generation Christians.

Night after night I walked with them through the centuries and shared the stories of faithful men and women—their brothers and sisters—who had followed Christ in their day, and it became clear to them that the gospel they had heard and believed was the same one that Paul and Polycarp and Perpetua believed and died for. Theirs was the same faith that Luther defended and that Hudson Taylor had sailed to the other side of the world to preach in Chinese. These truths were found in God's Word, the Bible— the same Scripture that Tyndale put into English and Carey translated into Bengali was the book that their pastor preached from in Albanian.

When this reality took hold, light shown in their eyes and joy filled their faces! They had been told by family and friends that they were deceived and were part of a small cult of fellow fools who had drunk the same Kool-Aid. But now they saw that the church wasn't just the forty or fifty people gathered in an apartment sitting on fold-up chairs. Instead, they were inseparably part of something worldwide and wonderful. They were connected to the saving work that Jesus himself started across the centuries and across the world as he gathered—and is gathering—his own from every nation and generation! Meeting this "company of heroes" from church history put iron in their souls and gave them greater perspective to endure the persecution and ridicule they faced.

These first-generation Christians found strength for endurance in the company of "saints below and saints above, the Church in earth and heaven."[3] I, too, have been impacted by the stories and examples of those who have gone before—and their strides in running after Christ have quickened my own pace.

John Piper put it this way:

> What I have found . . . is that in my pastoral disappointments and discouragements there is a great power for perseverance

in keeping before me the life of a man who surmounted great obstacles in obedience to God's call by the power of God's grace. I need very much this inspiration from another age, because I know that I am, in great measure, a child of my times. . . . When you are surrounded by a society of emotionally fragile quitters, and when you see a good bit of this ethos in yourself, you need to spend time with people— whether dead or alive—whose lives prove there is another way to live.[4]

## Many Proofs

Out of the whole range of exceptional Christians that I know or know of, how could I possibly narrow the list here to twenty or so individuals? First, these are men and women I've had the opportunity to walk with and talk with and serve alongside. I worshiped with their churches, whether they met under a mango tree or in a beautiful stone edifice or secretly in the shadow of a mosque. I ate their food, enjoyed their music, explored their neighborhoods, and heard them pray. This gave me the chance to add color and texture to the narrative portraits I capture in my journal so that the reader, as much as is possible, can experience their stories—not just know the facts of them.

Second, my gospel heroes from the past would make up a long list indeed! But the ones I write about here are those whose lives and impact I've had the opportunity to trace during my travels. I share David McCullough's love for experiencing a place in order to give history-writing more of its physical and emotional dimension, seeing the past as *their* present—real people in real time in a real place. McCullough said:

> I couldn't possibly have written about people trying to dig the Panama Canal without going down there and feeling the humidity, the rain, and the heat. For Truman I had to see the places where he was in World War I, and to make the run he made through the Capitol on the night that Roosevelt

died. . . . Well, that run, it seemed to me, was one of the key moments in the whole story. Why was he running? Was he running toward something or away from something? Did he somehow guess that he was running to the presidency? It's a great moment. I wanted to see how long it would have taken him to make that run, to figure out which route he took, because he could have gone several ways, to see what would have been flashing by in his peripheral vision.[5]

Tracing paths my gospel heroes walked helps me bring the reader along for the run, to widen their peripheral vision of the past.

The exceptional quality about these heroes—whether past or present—that has strengthened and steadied me is how all of them have oriented their lives around the truth that Jesus really is alive. They are living, walking, witnessing reminders of the resurrection because they daily demonstrate that Jesus is personally and powerfully with them—working in them and through them and for them. By their willingness to go and risk and act in the reality of the resurrection, they live out the truth that "the kingdom of God does not consist in talk but in power" (1 Cor. 4:20). The resurrection of Jesus Christ is the foundation of their endurance, risk-taking, and death-defying joy. Their optimism doesn't come from wishful thinking but from the power of an endless life—both Christ's and ours in him.

This confident hope has also given needed reminders to me—in a thousand different ways and places—that the church is *not* in decline. It's easy to think otherwise. Our fears, our tears, our comforts, our brokenness all obscure our vision. Then there is the daily downpour of bad news—a news crawl that feeds our doubts so that sometimes we find ourselves whispering in our hearts what a tactless Gideon blurted openly, "If the Lord is with us, why then has all this happened to us? And where are all his wonderful deeds that our fathers recounted to us?" (Judg. 6:13). The God whom Gideon was questioning was indeed alive, personal, and present—and about to do even more "wonderful deeds" through this unlikely servant. And it is the same today.

## The Real Hero

I'm always amazed at God's choices in the book of Hebrews to illustrate enduring faith. The company of heroes in chapter 11 is an uneven and unlikely lot that ranges from Abraham the patriarch to Rahab the prostitute. That's because the chapter is not a gallery for displaying human greatness but rather one that magnifies God's grace. It's as if everyone in Hebrews 11 is pointing down the line to the next chapter to the *real* hero of the story, "looking to Jesus, the founder and perfecter of our faith" (Heb. 12:2). The heroes you will meet in this book are also pointing in that same direction. They are pointing to their risen King, who has all authority in heaven and on earth. Therefore, his kingdom has no borders. He is mighty to save across every geographic, religious, political, and ethnic barrier—in war and in peace, from preliterate animists to past post-Christian sophisticates. The heroes in this book reflect this gracious diversity. They come from many backgrounds and many nations. They are ordinary men and women who have an extraordinary Savior. They love the gospel and live in the integrity, boldness, and humility that flow from its daily grace.

This kind of gospel-centered humility is glory-giving, not glory-getting. The heroes in this book disdain puffery. Their work is quiet, steady, often dull, and occasionally dangerous. At times it is nation-shaking, but always it is Christ-magnifying. Still, though, knowing their reluctance to have attention drawn to themselves, I remember a conversation that Stephen Ambrose shared in his classic World War II history, *Band of Brothers*. As he was interviewing a veteran of many hard and closely fought battles, the old soldier said to Ambrose, "Now listen, whatever you do in this book, don't go making me into a hero." Ambrose replied, "I don't make heroes. I only write about them."[6]

# 1

# Facing Fear

## Sayid, Aaron, and Jillian (North Africa)

"So I say this very sobering word: God's plan is that his saving purpose for the nations will triumph through the suffering of his people, especially his frontline forces who break through the darkness of Satan's blinding hold on an unreached people."[1]

*John Piper*

"Only let your manner of life be worthy of the gospel of Christ, so that whether I come and see you or am absent, I may hear of you that you are standing firm in one spirit, with one mind striving side by side for the faith of the gospel, and not frightened in anything by your opponents. This is a clear sign to them of their destruction, but of your salvation, and that from God." (Phil. 1:27–28)

"The more you mow us down, the more we grow. The blood of Christians is seed."[2] Tertullian, a North African Christian, penned that famous taunt around the year 200. All-powerful Rome was waging a bloody campaign against Christians—a defenseless, vulnerable minority, law-abiding in all things save the worship of the emperor. It was the most uneven contest imaginable—like lambs among wolves. Yet, Tertullian pointed out that it wasn't working. Despite Rome's best efforts to stamp out this infant movement, Christians continued to multiply. With a nice touch of derision, he added, "We have filled all the places that belong to you—cities, islands, forts, towns, exchanges; the military camps themselves, tribes, town councils, the palace, the senate, the marketplace; we have left you nothing but your temples."[3]

Steady, pervasive growth and intense persecution character-ized the church in North Africa during Christianity's early cen-turies—and it's a good description of the church in North Africa today. Rome couldn't stop the gospel's advance then, and radical Islam can't now. That's not to say things are easy. It's a nearly 100 percent Muslim region that stretches from Libya to Morocco, and one of its chief exports in recent years has been fighters for the armies of ISIS, most coming from Tunisia and Morocco.[4] In short, the spiritual darkness and physical danger faced by Chris-tians here is real, but Jesus is calling and positioning messengers throughout the region to "go, stand and speak . . . all the words of this life" (Acts 5:20 KJV).

I want to introduce you to several such messengers in North Africa: Sayid, Aaron, and Jillian. Their courage—or better to say, the way they face fear and overcome it—has been a strong ex-ample to me. Their obedience is Christlike, for it has cost them much. Death threats, painful betrayals, jail bars, and the daily demands of disciple-making have all been part of that obedience. But in their obedience to keep going, standing, and speaking, my friends have seen new life springing up from hard ground.

Aaron told me one of the passages that has given him hope to endure despite setbacks and his own weakness is the parable of the farmer scattering seed. It's a window into how Christ is building his church in North Africa. Jesus said, "The king-dom of God is as if a man should scatter seed on the ground.

He sleeps and rises night and day, and the seed sprouts and grows; he knows not how. The earth produces by itself, first the blade, then the ear, then the full grain in the ear. But when the grain is ripe, at once he puts in the sickle, because the harvest has come" (Mark 4:26–29). The "seed" is the Word of God, the life-giving message of the gospel. Even though the farmer can't make the seed grow, he still has a vital part to play in planting abundantly.

The parable ends swiftly. In the weeks leading up to the harvest, time slows, like the mocking monotony of a ticking clock. The farmer pushes on in hope, but weighed down by work and waiting, and days so ordinary you could miss the opportunity in them. But then life stirs from the ground, and when it's full and fruitful, then the harvest is gathered.[5]

### Atlas Mountains, Somewhere South of Fez, Morocco
*January 10, 2014*

A coal fire glows orange and hot in the smoky corner of this little village house somewhere in the Atlas Mountains. Supper is done; tea has been poured. I'm sitting on a sheepskin, bundled against the chill air, along with two Berber families, who are listening and questioning intently as my friends share good news with them in Arabic. And since I can't contribute to the conversation, I'll just drink in the tea and the warmth and scribble a few lines.

Set out from Casablanca early for the drive to this mountain village, the ancestral home of a Moroccan brother named Sayid. He and our friends, Aaron and Jillian, are letting me travel with them in this corner of North Africa along the western edges of the Sahara. Aaron and Jillian have served Christ in this region for nearly a decade. I love this couple's simple trust in their God's sovereign care and control in all things, even when—especially when—things are out of their control. In their straightforward obedience to go and make disciples in hostile territory, they don't overanalyze or overestimate what *can't* be done. Rather, they focus on what *can* be done—and do it.

It's clear that Aaron and Jillian have a complete partnership, sharing in all the highs and lows of ministry here. Beneath Jillian's petite 5'2" stature is a woman of grit and grace. In ten years of marriage, she and Aaron have lived in twelve houses on three continents. But she's not just following her husband on this journey—she is following Christ. The Lord has used Jillian to lead many daughters of Mohammed to the Savior.

Sayid was the first fruit of Aaron's disciple-making ministry in North Africa—a beautiful beginning, for Sayid is himself a disciple-maker now. Sayid speaks Arabic as well as his Berber dialect but no English. And my Arabic is confined to what halting baby talk I can conjure out of my little *Lonely Planet* phrasebook. But Sayid was delighted that I had learned *qahua*, the Arabic word for "coffee." When we stopped for a bite to eat, Sayid was eager to introduce me to Moroccan coffee called *nous-nous*, Arabic for "half-half." It is a perfect parfait—rich espresso topped with frothed cream and served in a shot glass.

Our road took us into the foothills of the Atlas range, and we broke up the long, cramped drive at Volubilis—the ruins of what was once an important Roman city on the edge of the empire. While exploring, I came across mosaics that were nearly two thousand years old. The images of lions and leopards are reminders that one of Volubilis's chief exports was wild animals for the gladiator games in the arenas of Carthage and Rome. It seems that because of its remoteness, Volubilis became something of a city of refuge for persecuted Christians in the late Roman period—and remained a center of Christianity until the early 700s, when Islamic armies put this city under the sword.

It was good to share the time together and to climb the ruins and imagine the Roman legions that once marched here. But daylight soon slipped away, and I had to make a reluctant retreat because we still had a lot of road ahead of us.

In Sayid's village with Aaron and Sayid

Reached Sayid's village after nightfall. His family welcomed us to their home, a typical Moroccan village house with thick mud-walled rooms flanking a courtyard open to the stars. Aaron and Jillian have visited Sayid's family often, but the fact that this time the women allowed Jillian to help in the kitchen was something of a breakthrough in their letting her enter their lives; so Jillian happily pitched in with Amina and Aziza as they prepared couscous. This meal is practically a sacrament here among the Berbers. We feasted together on the couscous, along with bread as big as a drumhead, called *hobs beldi,* and washed it down with continuous cups of mint tea.

Afterwards, we gathered around a little coal stove, the only heat source outside of the kitchen's earth oven. For the past hour, Sayid has been witnessing to his sister, sister-in-law, brother, and nephews. Aaron also shares of Christ in Arabic, and Sayid takes the message further in their Berber dialect, for Sayid and his family are Berber of the a-Mazighri, a family of North African tribes that stretch from here to Libya. Sayid is the only Christian in his family, the only Christian in his hometown. Together they spoke with compassion and urgency of Christ alone—until the last of the fire, the last of the day.

## Casablanca, Morocco
### *January 11, 2014*

I woke this morning in Sayid's village with the help of a pesky rooster. The air was cold, and in the distance morning light fingered through a gray sky and touched the distant mountains. In the early light, I found Sayid out sitting near the well drinking in the Word. This is his source. This is what fuels his endurance, his preaching, his counsel, his heart. Sayid has been in the faith for six years. Before that, he was a brick mason with a fifth-grade education. But during these six years, Sayid has walked with the Lord and filled his days and his heart with God's Word. I thought of the passage in Jeremiah, "Your words were found, and I ate them, and your words became to me a joy and the delight of my heart, for I am called by your name" (Jer. 15:16).

Before setting out for Casablanca, we had a visit from the local police chief. His name was Hussein, but I prefer to call him Barney Fife. It seems that since Sayid was arrested three years ago for the "crime" of sharing the gospel, the police try to keep track of him whenever they can. It was just a routine hassle. Barney was just doing his job—and to have a real, live ex-con in town along with several of his foreign accomplices likely spiced up an otherwise boring beat. Barney called in our names and passport numbers to the police headquarters in Fez; so while he finished up the report, we took a walk.

For Sayid this place holds many emotions. This is the mountainside where he was born, and from the mosque in the center of the village to every house and footpath in between, this is home. Here he first tasted new life in Christ. Here he first felt the sharp slap of rejection, but also here he first embraced the fellowship of suffering with the One who also came to his own, and his own received him not.

What's clear is when Christ lit the candle of Sayid's life, he couldn't conceal it. "A city set on a hill cannot be hid." The day Sayid was baptized, he sent a group message to over one hundred people—everyone in his phone contact list! It said simply, *"Walit Masihi"* (I have become a Christian). In this country, this was like asking to be killed, but Sayid did not have a death wish—he has a living hope. In fact, his old life was the real death sentence. Now in Christ he has never been more alive—Sayid has a life that no man can ever take away![6]

My brothers have taught me so much about fear and faith and risk. Aaron told me that when Sayid was put in jail three years ago, Aaron was in the grip of fear over it. He said that for him the only way to break fear's chokehold was to pray and then go out immediately and tell someone about Jesus—and so that's what Aaron did. In the name of Jesus, demons are cast out—and in the name of Jesus, fear is cast out too.

After the police report was completed, we said our goodbyes to Sayid's family and set out for Casablanca. Made good time on the unusually fine roads here and reached Casablanca by early afternoon. Gathered for worship with the house church that Sayid pastors. Before the fellowship around the Word, though, we had fellowship around the table. It was an amazing meal called *pastille*. It's a perfect pie of honey, almonds, caramelized onions, and pulled chicken, infused with a baker's dozen spices from saffron to cinnamon, all in a flaky, crunchy crust. We made short work of this Moroccan manna!

After our meal, one of the brothers shared his testimony. Kamal's first exposure to the gospel was through Christian satellite TV. The one thing that stood out to him was hearing Christians praying for all people—whereas a Muslim's standard prayer was for Allah to kill all non-Muslims. He saw a way of love and grace that led straight to Christ. He said the word *salvation* appears nowhere in the Koran, whereas the Bible is all about salvation. So Kamal believed on Jesus, the Messiah, and prayed to him in the only place he knew to pray—the mosque! He had never met another Christian, until one day at the café where he was a waiter he greeted a man with the salutation "peace and grace."

The standard Arabic greeting is usually only *salam* (peace), but Kamal said "peace and grace." This man, whose name was Mohammed and who also was a believer, said, "Are you a Christian?" Kamal said he was and that he prayed to Christ in the mosque. Mohammed said, "No. You don't need to go to the mosque to pray. You can pray anywhere, anytime because Christ is in you. And you don't need to clean yourself by the ceremonial washing because Christ has forever washed you by his blood." Later these two new-found brothers baptized each other in the ocean near Casablanca.[7]

Kamal's brother-in-law, Hasan, also shared his story. When the September 11 attacks occurred in the United States and thousands of innocent people were murdered in the name of Islam, he rejected Islam in his heart. Later, when Kamal shared Christ with him, Hasan immediately believed the gospel!

It was beautiful to see not just solitary believers but families—husbands, wives, children—worshiping Christ together. I felt like I saw twenty centuries slip away and was seeing a page from the book of Acts lived out.

After the testimonies and Sayid's message, they sang with much joy—and I was finally able to join in. I couldn't sing in Arabic, but I can clap in Arabic! As the psalmist said, "Clap your hands, all peoples! Shout to God with loud songs of joy!" (Ps. 47:1). And so we did. Singing songs of redeeming, steadfast love. Light has dawned! The Son has risen!

### Rabat, Morocco
### *January 12, 2014*

Up early for the drive to the bus station to send off two Peruvian missionaries. Aaron calls Cesar and Joel the "Gospel Pilgrims." About a year ago Aaron sent out an appeal to his friends in Peru for two men to come help him and Sayid respond to the thousands of requests for Bibles that they receive each year. Aaron said, "Send me two men who have a reputation for evangelism."

Cesar, a youth pastor, and Joel, an assistant pastor, responded. With the blessing of their churches, they were sent to people who have never once heard the gospel, seen a Bible, or met a Christian. Aaron and Sayid have poured much prayer and preparation to get Cesar and Joel to this day. These two Peruvians are reminders to me that missions is no longer from "the West to the rest." As Christ is bringing men and women to himself from every nation, so he is also sending them out to every nation!

Sending off the "Gospel Pilgrims"

Joel and Cesar are headed south, deep into the Atlas range to personally respond to requests for New Testaments and to share the gospel along the way to whoever will listen. Sitting in on their briefings the other day as they spread out a map on the floor and went over the routes and logistics, I thought of something Ernie Pyle wrote in a wartime dispatch: "A map is as common a piece of equipment among front-line officers as a steel helmet."[8] Maps and missions have gone together, I imagine, since Paul and Barnabas spread out a leather one. It's the geography of kingdom advance, where vision, prayer, and shoe leather come together.

Cesar and Joel have six months of Arabic language study, a backpack of New Testaments, and a joyful confidence in Christ their captain. Like soldiers advancing, Cesar and Joel have no idea where they will spend the night. All they know is that Jesus is in them and with them and for them—and that's enough. So in Spanish, English, and Arabic, we prayed over them, recalling David's praise in Psalm 140:7: "O LORD, my Lord, the strength of my salvation, you have covered my head in the day of battle." God, go before my brothers. Strengthen their hearts for the unknown days, the uncertain nights.

Aaron seemed deep in thought after our goodbyes. He told me that in times like this there's a constant battle in his heart "between the words of fear and the words of God."

Went back to Aaron and Jillian's home afterwards. This is a morning to rest and repack, getting ready for the long road to Marrakesh and beyond. Jillian made up a fine French press, and we had coffee and a chance to talk about her own journey of faith and fear and surpassing grace.

Jillian is a busy wife and mother of three; but her home, her heart, and her hands are always open—reaching, winning, and discipling the women around her. Her sincere love for her Muslim neighbors earns her space to ask searching questions, as she did recently when she asked a Moroccan mother, "How would you feel if your son completely gave himself to and completely dedicated himself to the teachings of Koran and Mohammed?" She answered that she would be afraid that he might become a jihadist, which is a real possibility because terror cells in Europe and ISIS ranks in Syria are filled with Moroccans.[9] Jillian replied that she, on the other hand, would be happy for her son to be completely dedicated to the teachings of Christ, wherever that might take him. The Muslim mom answered with sobering silence as the ground beneath her faith began to shake. This conversation reminded me of something Charles Spurgeon said long ago: "He who religiously obeys Mahomet [Mohammed] may yet be doing grievous moral wrong; but it is never so with the disciple of Jesus: obedience to Jesus is holiness."[10]

Jillian admitted that sometimes, especially in their first years in North Africa, fear paralyzed her. Some of the fear was her own, but some she caught from others in the missionary community. There was fear *of* man and fear *from* man. Jillian told me an interesting story that became a turning point for her in facing her fears during their first years in Morocco. She wanted the friendship, counsel, and input of older, veteran missionary wives; so she reached out to one of them, and they began taking early morning walks together. One morning as they were chatting about kids and life, the veteran missionary said, "Lately I've been having some good, heart-to-heart talks with J." Jillian thought to herself, "Jay? Her husband's name is Robert. Who is Jay?" Finally, she couldn't keep her question in any longer and said, "Who is Jay?" The veteran missionary stopped in her tracks in the middle of the quiet street where they were walking. In a whisper with an edge she said, "Jesus." Jillian was stunned and said, "If we can't even say the name of Jesus, what are we doing here?" And that was the end of their morning walks. The missionary was offended, and other missionary families labeled Jillian and Aaron as "confrontational." They were people to avoid because "they are going to get us kicked out."

This added isolation has been hurtful, but it's also helped them to focus on why they are here—to make the saving work known of the One whose name is above every name. She decided that whispering inside self-made, Jericho-high walls was no way to live, no way to point others to Jesus. This has by no means removed fear and pain from her path. Elisabeth Elliot once wrote: "To be a follower of the Crucified means, sooner or later, a personal encounter with the cross."[11] Over the years, like a living sacrifice, Jillian has had many encounters with the cross. One was the time that they were betrayed by an infiltrator, and a picture of Aaron, Sayid, and others baptizing a Moroccan believer was given to the police and put on the front page of the national newspaper. Even in this hard situation, Jillian found a silver lining. She said, "At least the whole country—even the king!—got to see that there are actual real, live Moroccan Christians!" Still, it was a time of great uncertainty. But Jillian's most painful encounter with the cross was when their entire family was featured on an Islamic terrorist site, complete with photographs of her children and threats upon their lives. She felt so violated and so vulnerable and so angry, and suddenly in this dark, dark valley, Christ, who took all our sin upon himself and gave us all his righteousness instead, exchanged her hate and fear with his love and peace. Only transforming grace can explain how she could forgive—and even pray for—those terrorists.

Jillian is clearly leaning hard on Christ, and he is helping her stand. Her fearless and faithful one is with her. Always.

Aaron and Jillian

## Marrakesh, Morocco

*January 13, 2014*

This afternoon we all set out for Marrakesh to respond to Bible requesters and to fellowship with some bands of believers scattered further south. A Moroccan brother named Marwan joined us. Marwan's journey from Islam to Christ is one of amazing grace. His steadiness and courage remind me so much of his mentor, Sayid. The two of them have led the way in the first ever in-country Christian radio broadcast. Their "studio" is simple and mobile and reaches listeners across North Africa as far as Libya. The broadcast provides opportunities for more online Bible requests, and the call-in programs elicit a full range of responses from sincere questions to daily death threats.

Our road out of Casablanca skirted the Atlantic briefly, but as we continued southward, the land changed—the terrain, the trees, even the sky changed. To the west, the late sun looked old and red, veiled in a cloud of fine dust. By the time we stopped for fuel and coffee, it was clear we were on the edge of the Sahara—on just a corner of a desert the size of the United States!

Reached Marrakesh in the evening. The night was cold, but we warmed ourselves with laughter and good coffee. Met for a Bible study with several brothers and sisters tonight. I was particularly blessed by the testimony of one sister. Fatima is from the far south in the Sahara. Her mother is a devout Muslim, but her father was neither a good Muslim nor a good husband; and by the time Fatima was fourteen, she was a convinced atheist. She went to law school and surprisingly had a professor there who wanted his students to research the differences in the legal systems of countries who based law on the Bible and those who based law on the Koran. But it was hard to do the assignment justice since there were no Bibles in the library and only one foreign student had a copy of the dangerous book. Frustrated that she could keep the borrowed Bible for only a few days, Fatima went online to see if she could somehow obtain her own copy. She found an internet site that offered a Bible, and, as a result, she met with Marwan and Aaron at a café where they gave her a copy. Over the course of several months, they and Jillian patiently and humbly answered her questions about the Bible. However, when Fatima asked questions about Islam at her law school, she was told, "Do not ask such questions. To even ask shows you are on the path to becoming a *kafir* (an infidel)—someone who is deserving of beheading."

The contrast between the Christian and the Muslim responses to questions could not have been greater—like the difference between light and darkness. Eventually, Fatima attended a church meeting, where she was struck by the sense of family among them, by the ordering of their lives around the Bible, and by their singing! Jillian spent countless hours with her, studying the Scriptures together and pointing her to Jesus. Two years ago, Fatima believed! She has told her family and has suffered much by their rejection and their accusations that she is mentally unstable. But my sister's confidence in Christ as the only Savior is strong, and the new life he has given her no one can ever take away. I thought of the passage in the Psalms: "When my father and my mother forsake me, then the LORD will take me up" (Ps. 27:10 KJV).

Also at the Bible study was a dear old gentleman named Ghafur. Over fifty years ago, Ghafur was a soldier sent to the Middle East during a time of war. One day he met a man in the street who was desperately searching for food for his family. Ghafur knew where he could get some supplies, so he got the food and accompanied the man back to his home, where the man's wife said with joy and relief, "We prayed to God in the name of Jesus, and he has heard our prayers!"

Over the years, Ghafur never forgot the gratitude of these Christians—nor the fact that when they prayed in Jesus's name, they got answers. Fifty years later, Ghafur was working as a security guard at a supermarket and saw a man waiting in the parking lot reading a book. That man was Aaron. "What are you reading?" Ghafur asked. "It's the New Testament," Aaron replied. "I heard of this book many years ago. Can I have one?" Ghafur asked. Aaron gave it to him and asked him to read the Gospel of Matthew. The next time Ghafur saw Aaron, he told him that he had read the entire New Testament and wanted to know more. After meeting with Aaron and coming to an understanding of the gospel, like the Christians he met decades earlier, Ghafur prayed in Jesus's name. Jesus set his sovereign love on my brother and made him new—and he told everyone! As a result, his family rejected him, and his wife left him. During our prayer time, Ghafur praised God for his new brothers and sisters. When Sayid asked for favorites during the singing, Ghafur's request was his testimony: "I Have Decided to Follow Jesus" . . . no turning back. They have a verse of this song in Arabic that we don't have back home: "If I'm put in chains, or go to prison, no turning back, no turning back."

## Southern Morocco
### *January 15, 2014*
Early yesterday morning took the highway south through a barren land of desert scrub dotted with mud-baked villages and tinted with colors of ochre, pale pink, and burnt tangerine, all under a sapphire sky. It's no surprise that great painters from Delacroix to Matisse were inspired by the palette and light of this wonderland. The mighty Atlas Mountains framed the horizon, spreading a curtain of snow and stone to wall off the sea of sand beyond it. Somewhere out there beyond them, Cesar and Joel are working. Got a quick call from them to let us know they are well and the Word is getting out. The Word is getting out here, too. Along the way, Aaron took every opportunity to share the good news. Over the past several days I have seen him give New Testaments and other gospel literature to many along the highways and hedges. He said that back in the States he is thought of as a Muslim "expert." He chuckles at that. He says he's just telling

people about Jesus—wherever they are and whoever they are. Islam is, in his words, "just another façade for lost people who are trying to save themselves."

Reached Agadir on the coast in late afternoon and gathered to worship with a little house church that meets in the shadow of a minaret. Just a few doors down from the mosque, we worshiped Jesus.

Some missionaries have criticized Aaron and Sayid for encouraging believers to gather and to share their faith, saying that they are putting Moroccan Christians in danger. Aaron told me, "Before these believers heard the gospel, they were on their way to hell—how could they be in worse danger than that?" If these Christians were taught to fear from the beginning, from their first breath of new life, they would likely remain silent. But my brothers and sisters share their faith with prayerful boldness because that's how it was shared with them. When they tell their good news to friends, they are like the woman in the parable of the lost coin whose invitation to her neighbors was simply winsome: "Come. Rejoice with me!" (see Luke 15:8–10).

This morning we huddled for prayer before setting out to the seaside for meetings with people who have requested New Testaments online. Thousands of these requests come in every year. There is always the possibility that the person asking to meet will turn out to be a member of the secret police, but Aaron's number one priority here is not avoiding deportation. Making disciples trumps even his visa. Sayid's and Marwan's risk is even greater—they know from experience they could be arrested. Yet they all live in the moment, where risk and joy are all one because Jesus is near. They are not "Walter Mitty" Christians, merely imagining all the heroic things they have done or will do. They know that bountiful sowing brings life, and so they go and give and serve and speak in the name of Jesus.

We divided so as to keep separate, staggered appointments at different cafés just off the boardwalk. While Sayid and Aaron had their meetings, and Jillian and Fatima theirs, I joined Marwan. We met a university student named Ali, who had never seen a Bible before but wanted one. Marwan was a first, too—the first Moroccan Christian Ali had ever met. We talked for an hour. Ali spoke some English; so I was able to join in the conversation and answer questions he had such as "Do Christians worship three gods?" "Why did Jesus have to suffer?" and "How can a man have a relationship with God?"

While we all grabbed lunch after our meetings, Marwan told us he had received an anonymous call threatening to turn him into the police for distributing gospel literature. He shrugged it off. If threats like that stopped them, they would have quit long ago. Before we were done, Aaron got a call from Cesar and Joel. They had given out many New Testaments and had even been invited to several homes, where they shared the gospel. But they added that local radio stations were reporting that Peruvians were distributing dangerous literature in the towns in that region.[12]

Late afternoon we set out for the ancient walled city of Taroudant in hopes of reaching it before nightfall. There's no church here and no known Christians. But several there have asked for Bibles, and so we go. A walled city is a fitting picture of the situation all across North Africa. The sheer scale of the walls of opposition and the doors of opportunity are overwhelming. But my dear friends here—and other such gospel foot soldiers— are the everyday, everywhere infantry that God is using to move the boundaries of his kingdom into more and more hearts. I share Ernie Pyle's affection for those on the front lines in every danger and season. He wrote, "I love the infantry because they are the underdogs. They are the mud-rain-frost-and-wind boys. They have no comforts, and they even learn to live without the necessities. And in the end they are the guys that wars can't be won without."[13]

By the time we reached the city, dusk was settling in its streets and last light touched the top of its battlements. And now, before entering the walls of this Jericho, we believe the words of Christ our captain as he walks among his troops here on the front lines, giving us his strong, personal promises that cheer our hearts:

"Fear not, for I have redeemed you;
    I have called you by name, you are mine.
When you pass through the waters, I will be with you; . . .
when you walk through the fire you shall not be burned,
    and the flame shall not consume you.
For I am the LORD your God . . .
    your Savior. . . .
you are precious in my eyes,
    and honored . . . I love you. . . .
Fear not, for I am with you. . . .
bring my sons from afar
    and my daughters from the end of the earth,
everyone who is called by my name,
    whom I created for my glory." . . .
"You are my witnesses." (Isa. 43:1–7, 10)

# 2

# The Glory of the Cross

## Samuel Zwemer (Bahrain and Jerusalem)

"Do you not understand that we overcome the accuser on the ground of the blood of Christ? Nothing more, nothing less. That is how we win. It is the only way we win. This is the only ground of our acceptance before God. That is why we can never get very far from the cross without distorting something fundamental, not only in doctrine but in elementary discipleship, faithful perseverance, obedience, and spiritual warfare against the enemy of our souls. If you drift far from the cross, you are done. You are defeated."[1]

*D. A. Carson*

"If faithfully, fearlessly, sympathetically, we preach Christ crucified, he can make the stumbling block of the cross a stepping stone for the Muslims into his kingdom. There is no other way into that kingdom than the way of the cross."[2]

*Samuel Zwemer*

As I write in my study, the wall before me is lined with shelves of books and a scattering of swords, helmets, and medals. Among them is a bronze cross stamped with *Treuen Kriegern*—"to faithful warriors." It was awarded to all Prussian soldiers who took part in the brief, decisive war with Austria in 1866. The interesting thing about this particular medal is that after the Austrian defeat, the Prussian leader Bismarck had the captured cannons melted down to make these victory medals! For the Austrians, their very weapons had been seized and turned into marks of their defeat; but for the "faithful warriors," it was their badge of honor, their sign of total victory.

Similarly, the story behind this bronze cross is a little picture of the stunning reversal at Calvary. The cross of Christ was both the instrument of his death and the way by which he forever crushed the power of sin and death. By Jesus's cross and empty tomb, we are "made alive together with him, having forgiven us all our trespasses, by canceling the record of debt that stood against us with its legal demands. This he set aside, nailing it to the cross. He disarmed the rulers and authorities and put them to open shame by triumphing over them in him" (Col. 2:13–15). With one stroke, Jesus at once delivered his people and devastated his enemies. Spurgeon said, "It seemed as if hell were put into his cup; he seized it and at one tremendous draught of love, He drank damnation dry."[3]

So, the first century's most offensive symbol of shame and defeat became the symbol of glory for the followers of the Christ of the cross. John Stott pointed out how important the symbol of the cross was to these first-century believers:

> It was out of loyalty to him that his followers clung so doggedly to this sign. . . . We must not overlook their remarkable tenacity. They knew that those who had crucified the Son of God had subjected him to "public disgrace" and that in order to endure the cross Jesus had had to humble himself to it and to "scorn its shame." Nevertheless, what was shameful, even odious, to the critics of Christ, was in the eyes of his followers most glorious. They had learnt that the servant was not greater than the master, and that for

them as for him suffering was the means to glory. More than that, suffering *was* glory, and whenever they were "insulted because of the name of Christ," then "the Spirit of glory" rested upon them.[4]

Samuel Zwemer, the Apostle to Islam

"Remarkable tenacity" to the cross well describes the gospel labors of Samuel Zwemer (1867–1952). The glory of the cross was the message he clearly, unashamedly, and lovingly took to the heart of the Muslim world. "If the Cross of Christ is anything to the mind, it is surely everything—the most profound reality and the sublimest mystery. One comes to realize that literally all the wealth and glory of the gospel centers here."[5] What Zwemer said of the cross came from a deep understanding of the gospel—the one central message from the one sovereign God who alone can save. It was the driving motivation of Zwemer's first book, written in the 1890s in Arabia (where he had to wrap his hand in a towel to keep sweat from smearing the ink), to his last books and sermons—among them an address to students in 1946 at what would be the first Urbana Conference for mobilizing a new generation of missionaries.

> Are we here at this Convention deeply conscious that we have an essential message, a message that means life to those who accept it or death to those who reject it? Can we state this message in language so plain that all can understand its import? It is time that a protest be made against the misuse of the word "evangelism." It has only one etymological, New Testament, historical, and theological connotation; namely, to tell the good news of One who came to earth to die on the cross for us: who rose again and who ever lives to intercede for those who repent and believe the Gospel. To evangelize is to win disciples, to become fishers of men, to carry the Gospel message directly to all the nations.[6]

Sixty years earlier, Samuel Zwemer had, in a sense, sat where those students sat. He was challenged to give his life in service to Christ and the nations when he was a student at Hope College in his hometown of Holland, Michigan. After Zwemer committed his life to missions, his mother told him that when he was a baby, whenever she put him in his cradle, she would pray over him, asking God to call her son to be a missionary—and God answered her prayers.

Zwemer set his compass for one of the hardest, most neglected places on the planet: Arabia, the epicenter of Islam, a hostile place both physically and spiritually. After language study in Beirut, Zwemer reached the Arabian Peninsula in 1890. Maps and demographic information were sketchy, but Zwemer was aided by the help of Major General F. T. Haig, whose expeditions into the interior and his love for missions gave him special insight into the situation on the ground. Haig's unadorned assessment was just what the young pioneer needed. The general said, "In one degree or another, all Arabia is open to the Gospel. It is as much open to it as the world generally was in Apostolic times; that is to say, it is accessible to the evangelist at many different points, at all of which he would find men and women needing salvation, some of whom would receive his message while others would reject it and persecute him. . . . There is no difficulty about preaching the Gospel in Arabia if men can be found to face the consequences."[7] Samuel Zwemer was such a man.

In 1896 Zwemer married equally intrepid Amy Elizabeth Wilkes, an English nurse who was serving in Baghdad. The two of them made Bahrain, an island on the eastern shores of Arabia, their home and mission base. Together they were a gospel force: speaking of Christ at every opportunity, distributing Bibles, starting the first school for girls, providing care for orphans, and, with a growing team, opening the first hospital on the island. They also coauthored a book about Arabia written especially for children, an extensive pictorial introduction to the geography, culture, and gospel needs of Arabia. It was remarkable for the times and, I believe, a reflection of their complete partnership in the work that their names are side by side on the cover of *Topsy-Turvy World: Arabia Pictured for Children*.

But Bahrain was also where Samuel and Amy suffered the deepest loss of their lives. In July 1904, dysentery swept through the community. In the space of a week, the Zwemers buried their firstborn, a seven-year-old daughter named Amy, and their youngest daughter, three-year-old Ruth. Years later Zwemer pulled back the curtain on their grief, and in doing so, showed the depths of their sorrow and their worship as they buried their precious ones. Zwemer said that his wife wrote their daughters' epitaph, which said simply, "Worthy is the Lamb that was slain to receive riches."[8]

A few years ago I was traveling in the Middle East, bound for Jerusalem. Along the way, I made a brief stop in Bahrain to find the graves of the little Zwemer girls. I wanted to see the place where the claims of the cross and the hope of the resurrection met for Samuel and Amy Zwemer. I also wanted to see glimpses of gospel work there today.

## Bahrain
### *March 9, 2015*

As the sun sinks into the western wastelands of Arabia, the silhouetted cityscape could pass for a sci-fi movie set—the rocketship-shaped skyscraper across from my hotel looks ready to launch, and nearby glass and steel high-rises designed like sailboats lean into the sea breeze as night falls over Bahrain.

I reached this little island-kingdom today. Bahrain, like a docking station on the Death Star, is tethered on the west to Saudi Arabia by a sixteen-mile-long causeway. Across the gulf to the east is Iran. So, Bahrain is positioned between the two heavyweights of Islam: the Saudis and the Iranians—Sunni and Shia. Geography is destiny. The majority of Bahraini Muslims are Shia, but they are ruled by Sunni Arabs. Being a long-time seafaring trading stop on the Persian Gulf and one of the oil-rich city-states along eastern Arabia, Bahrain is a destination for workers and students from the region and from across south Asia. This diverse society is all packed on a cluster of desert islands collectively the size of Austin's city limits.

Through a friend of a friend, I met with Bill and Jeana, veteran missionaries who have spent nearly thirty years serving in Bahrain. They gave good insight to help me understand the situation on the ground. All of Arabia is hard. Some places are violently hostile to the gospel, but among the nations of the peninsula, Bahrain is one of the freest. The ethnic diversity and religious divide between Shia and Sunni have forced a bit more tolerance, which has opened the door a bit wider for Christians. Plus, there is a still recognition of the role that Christians had in providing the first schools and hospitals more than a century ago. In fact, Bill and his wife came to Bahrain to serve in connection with the American Mission Hospital, which is the hospital started by Samuel and Amy Zwemer.

I was delighted that Bill and Jeana could show me around the hospital. Of course, a lot has changed since 1903. The one photograph I've seen of the original structure shows a simple, serviceable two-story hospital building, complete with a camel in the barren background. Today, the hospital is a modern, multistory facility that straddles a busy highway choked with cars instead of camels. A sky bridge connects the two sides of the hospital. Bill showed me the chapel, and a display that highlights the hospital's history and Zwemer's work. To me, the most striking feature was a window formed in the shape of a cross, which is clearly seen by all on the outside—and light-giving to all on the inside!

Afterwards, with Bill's help, we found the keeper of the key to the Old Christian Cemetery. The dusty half-acre is enclosed with a high wall, although several years ago, a fanatic got in and smashed crosses and headstones. The damage was patched, and the place is well-kept. In fact, after opening the gate for us, the caretaker went over the sandy ground with a broom, sweeping fallen palm fronds and seagull droppings off the graves. Crosses stood stark against the brown, barren ground. Buried here are sailors, soldiers, diplomats—mostly British—who died in service here. But there are also many small graves of children, who were most vulnerable to the epidemics that swept through the island with fearful unpredictability.

Some of the gospel pioneers are buried here, too, including Dr. Marion Thoms, the first female medical doctor in Bahrain, who died while saving others. Near her grave, I found the graves of Amy and Ruth Zwemer, who died within days of each other and were buried together. It's a lonely spot. Zwemer wrote little about this in his memoirs beyond recording the words of worship his wife wrote for their daughters' epitaph, as they entrusted their little lambs into the strong, scarred hands of the Lamb who is worthy. When Zwemer was in his eighties, the old veteran returned here for the last time. In looking at his daughter's graves he said, "If we should hold our peace these very stones would cry out for the evangelization of Arabia."[9]

Grave of Amy and Ruth Zwemer

Because of the cross and empty tomb, their sorrow upon sorrow was also hope upon hope, for in Christ there is grace upon grace. Like the hospital window I saw today, the cross-shaped gospel brought light to their darkest days—and it brings life to all who put their trust in the Lamb.

## Jerusalem
### March 11, 2015

Footsore from a day of exploring and my mind racing to write, I found a sign with three welcome words on it: Christian Coffee

Shop. The place sits in the shadow of the Tower of David, not far from Jaffa Gate. With cappuccino, carrot cake, and free Wi-Fi, it's an oasis indeed! A good time to mix coffee with ink.

Took a flight from Bahrain yesterday, reaching Amman long enough to poke around a bit and catch a few hours of sleep before setting out for Jerusalem early this morning. The Jordanian capital was not yet awake when I slipped out into open country to cross the Jordan at the Allenby Bridge. While not as miraculous as the time Joshua and the Israelites crossed here, with all the barriers, checkpoints, twists, and turns between the Jordanian and Israeli sides, I felt like the waters parted when I finally cleared the last checkpoint. Thankfully, I'm living out of my backpack these days; so I only have myself to keep up with. Connected with another driver on the West Bank side and headed through the Judean hill country, which is greening under the breath of spring. Seeing Jericho, the Dead Sea, and signs for Hebron and Bethel, I felt like we were driving through a Bible encyclopedia. Everything is so close here.

Went on to the Mount of Olives. A flood of scenes came to mind on this holy ground as I read aloud Luke's account of the triumphal entry and triumphal ascension, both of which began here. Between them there was Gethsemane's dark night, where prayers and tears, blood and betrayal mingled. How much he suffered to save me!

Jerusalem: "On this mountain. . . . He will swallow up death forever."

51

Despite the gaggle of tour groups and all the churches and chapels staking their claims along the face of the Mount of Olives, seeing the Kidron Valley with Jerusalem atop Mount Moriah was a dream come true. There on that ridge, before there was any city here, Abraham offered his son, but God provided a substitute. And here, centuries later, God offered his Son—who was the substitute! This little ridge, this chosen place, is the greatest mountain in the world—not Everest, Denali, or Kilimanjaro. As Isaiah said, "And he will swallow up on this mountain the covering that is cast over all peoples, the veil that is spread over all nations. He will swallow up death forever" (25:7).

So with joy I walked on and entered the Dung Gate to pray at the remnant of the temple, the Western Wall. Access to the sacred wall is divided between men and women, and all men must have their heads covered to enter their courtyard. Little caps, *yarmulke*, were provided for those, like me, who were unprepared. And so I joined the men in praying—not with lamentations like the Jews around me, but with praise to the crucified, risen, returning King. His promise that the gospel would go out first here in Jerusalem and then "to the end the earth" is still unfolding. Unstoppable. *Lord Jesus, be magnified more and more until the whole earth is filled with your glory. May millions more proclaim, "Behold, this is our God; we have waited for him, that he might save us. This is the* LORD; *we have waited for him; let us be glad and rejoice in his salvation"* (Isa. 25:9).

Walked on to the Church of the Holy Sepulchre. The church is a sprawling structure that has endured the ravages of fire and war and at least one more devastating earthquake since the one that occurred as "the curtain of the temple was torn in two. . . . And the earth shook, and the rocks were split" (Matt. 27:51). This ancient edifice shelters the place of Jesus's death and resurrection. Both early church history and archeological evidence support the claim that here are the sites of Golgotha and the empty tomb.

The great doors to the ancient church must be nearly twenty feet tall and are of wood and iron, scarred by time and smoothed by pilgrims' hands. Each morning a Muslim key-keeper unlocks the church doors—a curious practice that dates back more than a century, necessitated by the bitter fighting among Christian groups over control of the holiest pilgrimage site of Christianity. The Muslim decree, known as the "Status Quo," forced a truce among the competing Syrian, Coptic, Greek, Ethiopian, Armenian, and Roman Catholic churches. It gave them joint access, but turned the key to the church over to a neutral Muslim key-keeper. I guess it's not surprising—religion is all about who has the best brand, who gets the naming rights. But the gospel—what Jesus did here—blows away all that kind of thinking because there is only one name that really matters—and that's his, "the name that is above every name" (Phil. 2:9).

Inside, the air was heavy with incense and echoed with the chant of monks. Within the church, the way to Golgotha was along a dark passage flecked with candlelight—the dim light matched the mood. When Jesus was crucified, it was likely on a small prominence in an abandoned limestone quarry outside the city walls. Much of that rocky rise has long since been removed, but a precious remnant of Calvary's rugged hill is enclosed within the church, and in places it can be seen behind glass. It was stunning to stand there. In a sense, I've been here before—at least I had a hand in this place. For here, as Isaiah said, "He was pierced for [my] transgressions, he was crushed for [my] iniquities" (53:5). I thought of Lancelot Andrewes's meditation:

> By Thy sweat bloody and clotted! Thy soul in agony,
> Thy head crowned with thorns, bruised with staves.
> Thine eyes a fountain of tears,
> Thine ears full of insults,
> Thy mouth moistened with vinegar and gall,
> Thy face stained with spitting,
> Thy neck bowed down with the burden of the Cross,

Thy back ploughed with the wheals and wounds of the
    scourge,
Thy pierced hands and feet,
Thy strong cry, Eli, Eli,
Thy heart pierced with the spear,
The water and blood thence flowing,
Thy body broken, Thy blood poured out—
Lord forgive the iniquity of Thy servant
And cover all his sin.[10]

Took my place in line to enter the tiny chapel that shelters the site where Jesus was buried and rose again. When my turn came, I stooped to enter the little chamber built over the place of Jesus's tomb. Inside, a stone marks the place where his body was laid. The marble slab is polished smooth by millions of hands and lips that have caressed that sacred spot. It was good to touch the place where the death of death occurred, for our faith is not tied to myth and make-believe. We have a real Savior who came to a real place in a real point in time—facts and history as hard as this stone.

As I came out of his tomb and worked my way out of the crowd, suddenly all the clutter and spectacle seemed to disappear. The angel's words, "He is *not here*! He is *not here*!" rang in my heart. That's all that matters. Though surrounded by the dark walls, dark priests, and busloads of tourists, nothing could distract me from worshiping him there, for my death-defeating King is full of life-giving life!

I think of those lonely little graves in Bahrain and of how only in Christ does hope rest over such hard ground and hard questions. These words have rehearsed this glorious anticipation in my mind and heart over and over:

Wake up, wake up
And listen for the trumpet-sound
For a dead man rose up from the ground!

Rise up, rise up
You dry bones in the dirt,
For the Son of God has risen up first!

Sown in weakness, raised in power
Sown in dust, death, and dishonor.
Raised immortal, never again to die.
Death is swallowed up by life.[11]

# 3

# The Character for Bravery

## Mei Li (China)

"Lucy looked along the beam and presently saw something in it. At first it looked like a cross, then it looked like an aeroplane, then it looked like a kite, and at last with a whirring of wings it was right overhead and was an albatross. . . . It called out in a strong sweet voice what seemed to be words though no one understood them. After that it spread its wings, rose, and began to fly slowly ahead. . . . No one except Lucy knew that as it circled the mast it had whispered to her, 'Courage, dear heart,' and the voice, she felt sure, was Aslan's, and with the voice a delicious smell breathed in her face."[1]

*C. S. Lewis*

Courage, like fear, is contagious—and both are cultivated in the company we keep. I've seen the impact of Mei Li's quiet leadership and contagious courage in growing the vision of her brothers and sisters in China for missions and mercy. But from the outset, painful rejection, persecution, and the daily cat-and-mouse pressure of gospel work in China have marked the path of her new life. But there has been joy, too, and steadying courage in the company of Jesus, who has been to her friend and brother, shepherd and shield, king and cross-bearer. Mei Li also drew courage from the lives of the pioneers who first brought the gospel to China. Early on she found that reading their biographies opened her eyes to the reality of the global work of God that she now had a place in. Their courage gave her courage. She has taken up the torch and is "surrounded by so great a cloud of witnesses," as these faithful ones have taken their places in the stands cheering her on as she reaches and disciples her people in this generation.

Once when I was traveling across a wide swath of China, our paths converged for a few days, giving me a rare opportunity to capture in my journal more of my friend's story told in motion. Mei Li is a foot soldier, an unlikely, anonymous hero in the kingdom's extraordinary advance in China—anonymous because "Mei Li" is a pseudonym used for security reasons, and unlikely because of the painful journey this naturally timid woman has endured. It is through such unlikely and unknown servants that Christ does his work. Mei Li can say with Paul, "But as servants of God we commend ourselves in every way: by great endurance, in afflictions, hardships, calamities, beatings, imprisonments, riots, labors, sleepless nights, hunger; by purity, knowledge, patience, kindness, the Holy Spirit, genuine love; by truthful speech, and the power of God; with the weapons of righteousness for the right hand and for the left; through honor and dishonor, through slander and praise. We are treated as impostors, and yet are true; as unknown, and yet well known; as dying, and behold, we live; as punished, and yet not killed; as sorrowful, yet always rejoicing; as poor, yet making many rich; as having nothing, yet possessing everything" (2 Cor. 6:4–10).

## Shanghai, China
### *August 17, 2014*

My room on the thirty-seventh floor puts me in the middle of a storm that has swept in over the dark city. Through the mist and a rain-spattered window, the gaudy lights of Shanghai run like watercolors. Boat lights blink in the Huangpu, and the skyline (like me) seems to be shutting down for the night. It's been a long, good first day here.

Shanghai riverfront

This morning crossed an old iron bridge that dates back to Hudson Taylor's time. Doubtless he often crossed this canal here during his time in Shanghai, although perhaps the only thing he would recognize now is the bend in the wide, meandering Huangpu. This river was his gateway to China. Back then, Westerners—missionaries, mariners, and merchants alike—stayed in this part of Shanghai. The embankment called the Bund and its wide promenade mark what was once the wall of the foreigners' settlement. It is still a magnet for foreigners—or at least tourists—and therefore a good place to connect with my friend in order to get lost in the crowd as we quietly lay our plans for the days ahead in a country where sometimes the walls have ears.

Met Mei Li along the Bund. She is what we would call an organizer in the underground church. Mei Li is a visionary and entrepreneur whose business is to be about our "Father's business." We have served together for at least a decade in the kingdom's advance in China, and she is one of the bravest women I know. While we talked, I noticed that a woman and her son were throwing live fish into the river. Why? Mei Li explained this Buddhist ritual. Buddhists will spend large sums of money at the fish market to "rescue" fish caught that morning and then return them to the river. While I am sure the fish are happy about this arrangement, it's not really about them—the amount spent and the fish being offered back into the circle of life is like money in the Bank of Heaven, righteous karma credit, which will help this woman when she dies to move up the ladder when she is reincarnated and, perhaps, be a rich woman—better yet, a rich man—or at least next time around not be moved back down a rung or two and be just another carp like the grateful ones who are getting a second chance this morning. Mei Li has seen such dark superstition many times, and her eyes glistened with sorrow to tell of it.[2]

Late afternoon Mei Li arranged for me to meet an old uncle—that is, an elderly leader in the house church movement. Uncle Zhao has known Mei Li for years, and since Zhao trusts her, he was willing to meet me and share his stories and counsel. There are few such men left. Thousands of pastors were executed by the Communists in the 1950s and '60s, and many thousands more died in prison—starved to death, worked to death, or beaten to death. Mr. Zhao went to prison back when he was in college. Two thousand other preachers in his province were also rounded up—only two hundred of them made it out alive. Uncle Zhao is now in his seventies but still going strong. He is an itinerant evangelist and teacher. We know him as Zhao, but he goes by other names in other places to help cover his tracks from the police and their informants. His life is given—doubtless to the last of it—to the advance of the gospel and the health of the church. He said the Lord did something special in the 1950s in building a truly Chinese church—one birthed in suffering and multiplied in persecution, but one that (like any church) can still lose its focus. Uncle Zhao voiced concerns about the detriment and divisions brought on by Western Christianity's money and methods. Zhao is a man who keeps his eyes on the prize. The remedy for the Chinese church, he said, is to not get distracted from the mission that continues to drive him after more than a half century: "Follow Christ. Lift up the cross!"

We urged Uncle Zhao to stay on and have supper with us, but he couldn't. He had a train to catch and believers to teach in other cities—Christians who know him by face, if not by name. Uncle must keep moving.

## On the Rail, Shanghai to Beijing
*August 18, 2014*

Took the bullet train to Beijing. Our train slips through miles of mist. Smooth. Effortless. This rail is a real silk road—and traveling at 190 miles per hour, I feel like Superman without the cape. This fast ride is a mirror of China's rapid rise. Long stretches of apartments and factories were, not long ago, squatty little villages. Where farmers' fields stood and water buffalos plowed, the land is now laced with asphalt and choked with truck traffic. It's as if everyone, all of a sudden, just decided to skip a century. China has changed, and the world is changing with her—adjusting to new realities in Asia and beyond.

But it's too early to think too much about geopolitics—and so I went in search of coffee. As I walked through the crowded cars, I thought of something the traveler Paul Theroux wrote from one of his many train trips. "Travel means living among strangers, their characteristic stinks and sour perfumes, eating their food, listening to their dramas . . . being always on the move towards an uncertain destination, creating an itinerary, inventing the trip, cobbling together a set of habits in order to stay sane, keeping out of trouble, and writing everything down in order to remember."[3]

With five hours before reaching the capital, it's a good time to take Theroux's advice and write more of my friend's story. Mei Li's life mirrors China's pace of change. When she was growing up, there were no grocery stores, no clothing shops—the government issued coupons for most everything, at least while the supplies lasted. Except for the party elites, it was a Communist utopia of scarcity, control, and fear. It was what Winston Churchill called "an equality of misery."

Mei Li's dad worked long hours, seven days a week; so she didn't see him much. She adored her mother and was fiercely protective of her younger sister, even facing down a gang of bullies that once threatened her. It was a pattern of life as she learned to mask her fear with a strong face—protect the weak, meet trouble head-on—even if her feet wanted to run the other way. I asked Mei Li to write in my journal the Chinese character for "bravery." I expected a single character—a few ink strokes of Mandarin. Instead, what she did revealed so much about her heart. She penned three of her favorite quotations:

"She wrote of brave character."

"If I had a thousand lives to give, I would give them all for China—no, for Christ!"—Hudson Taylor

"He is no fool who gives what he cannot keep to gain that which he cannot lose." —Jim Elliot

And one by William Borden, who turned his back on fame and fortune to take the gospel to China but died before he reached these shores. He had written in his Bible, "No reserves. No retreat. No regrets."

I had asked her to write the character for bravery—instead she wrote of brave character! With tears in her eyes, Mei Li said that these gospel trailblazers modeled Christlike courage for her and other Chinese believers. The fearful little girl who put on her game face and met trouble head-on hasn't changed that much—only now she isn't taking the lead. Christ is, and she's just following him—no regrets, no retreat.

## Beijing
### August 19, 2014

Took a look around Beijing today. With twenty-two million people stacked high, Beijing has a population density that's comparable to a crowded elevator. Mei Li and I went to the heart of it, exploring Tiananmen Square—a vast, China-sized plaza flanked with the monuments and muscle of the Communist Party. At one end is Mao's mausoleum where the corpse of modern China's godlike founder is on display in a glass case. Communists have this weird thing about pickling their supreme leaders in formaldehyde and painting them up like a mannequin—and then every few years when they start to rot, do it all over again. It's creepy. Lenin, Mao, Ho Chi Minh, and the father and son founding tyrants of North Korea are all on permanent display for their faithful followers to reverence. It's atheism's pathetic version of the resurrection. I'm thankful my Supreme Leader's tomb is empty!

History has been written, erased, and rewritten here. In Tiananmen Square in 1949, Mao announced the Communists' victory and the founding of the People's Republic of China; a massive portrait now hangs where he stood. Mao became the biggest mass murderer of the twentieth century, responsible for at least sixty million deaths—more than double that of Hitler and Stalin combined. Mao's greatest weapon was fear—for boundless terror is the best way to control hundreds of millions of people from cradle to grave. Mei Li was a little girl when Mao died; but fear, like his corpse, remained long afterwards.

When Mei Li was a teenager, a peaceful student demonstration burgeoned into a freedom movement right here in Tiananmen Square. The world was stunned by the courage of these students, and their rulers were threatened by it. So with a word, the army moved in, killing untold thousands of them. The square ran with blood—but all that has been cleaned up now. Inside China, history books have been cleaned up too, and internet searches for "Tiananmen Square Massacre" show "no results." Beyond all the Instagram moments and souvenir sellers, this place is filled with paranoia. The Communist Party is looking over its shoulder here, and the people know they are being watched.

Afterwards, took a taxi out to a showcase church near Beijing's Olympic Village. A government that can tell its people what they can eat and wear will also tell them what they can believe. And so, early on, the Communists organized state-approved churches, known as the Three-Self Patriotic Movement. Although there are many evangelical believers among the congregants and pastors, one of the cardinal doctrines for the registered church has always been loyalty to the state.

In the same year as the Tiananmen Square Massacre, Mei Li's mom got a Bible, and the two of them started attending the Three-Self church to try to start to understand what this book was all about. But there was no life at that church. No gospel. After two and a half years, they went to a cultic church called the Real Jesus Church; but Jesus (the real one) was not preached there either. After three more years Mei Li and her mom joined another group that reached out to them—but it was like jumping out of the frying pan and into the fire, for this, too, was a cult—an anti-Trinitarian, health-and-wealth cult.

For eight years, Mei Li wandered like a spiritual beggar searching for bread and was given only empty ritual and the husks of heresy. But Jesus had set his sovereign love on my sister, for a pastor from an unregistered church shared the gospel with her and her mom—and they immediately believed! They started attending a house church in their city, where they fed deeply on the Word, which fueled their love, fellowship, and mission more and more!

## Jin Shan Ling, Great Wall
*August 20, 2014*

This morning set out to see the Great Wall. The road took us through rugged, sharp, fang-like mountains that in ancient times served to light signal fires from the Great Wall to the Imperial City to summon the men to the defense of the realm. Cell towers have now replaced the burning beacons, and thankfully cable cars helped us scale the mountains and breach these fortressed walls, where once it took an entire army.

We explored an unreconstructed portion of the wall called Jin Shan Ling. The Great Wall, like the Great Pyramids, is one of the remaining wonders of the ancient world. Built over many centuries, snaking across some five thousand miles of China, it served to control and defend the western borders of the realm. The sheer scale of the Wall stretches both the imagination and body to grasp it—at times, we were climbing on all fours to do just that! From here I can count on one hand the number of people I see. It's quite a contrast from the crush of the capital yesterday, but this place gives me space to write and think more about Mei Li's journey.

Taking a rest in the ruins of an old watchtower along this stretch of The Great Wall. We have had an amazing climb, but with heart pounding and quads quivering, I have reached my limit. Tomorrow we set out for Mei Li's city to meet brothers and sisters there. I thought much about our conversation yesterday in Beijing. The steep, hard climb today has been like her own spiritual journey through dead religion and dangerous cults to new life—only to then face persecution, opposition, and deep pain. Mei Li's husband never understood her after she became a Christian and left her for another woman. Her life in Christ has been a battle from the start—and ministry, like a minefield. But like a good soldier, she keeps following her trusted Captain. Hudson Taylor wrote from this very land words that Mei Li lives out in the arena: "The work of a true missionary is work indeed, often very monotonous, apparently not very successful, and carried on through great and varied but unceasing difficulties."[4]

## Somewhere in Northern China
### August 22, 2014

Caught a flight from Beijing to Mei Li's city. Reached there this evening and went on to one of the Christian bookstores and cafés that Mei Li has started. While she caught up with her store manager, I ordered up a cappuccino.

When I first met Mei Li ten years ago, this was her dream: opening Christian bookstores. She was a pioneer in this effort. Reading solid Christian books was one of the things that helped deliver her from the heresies of the cultic churches she came out of, and so she wanted to turn her business and entrepreneurial drive into making Christian books available to strengthen other believers and to share good news.

These Christian bookstores, though under scrutiny, are legal in China. Their stock is somewhat limited but still includes works on Christian parenting, apologetics, and even biographies of Hudson Taylor and his fellow missionaries. Mei Li also has a good supply of well-bound Bibles for just ten yuan apiece (about a dollar and a half). She has also expanded her bookstores to include a coffee bar and Wi-Fi to attract college students. Ultimately, though, this isn't a place to buy books and cappuccinos—it's a place for God-seekers to get answers, a place to make disciples.

Afterwards, sat in on a back-room meeting with Mei Li and the team leaders of a ministry called Left Hand. In their culture, the left hand signifies the supporting and helping hand, and so theirs is a ministry of mercy to the unloved and unreached. They started this ministry in part to help their church regain its focus. Theological squabbles in the church were causing members to lose sight of their mission of loving mercy, doing justice, and walking humbly.

Like their spiritual ancestors, the China Inland missionaries, Left Hand is taking the gospel deep into China to people groups in Yunnan, Qinghai, and Inner Mongolia. Tonight, Jiang, a house church pastor in this city and one of the Left Hand leaders, brought back his report from the south, where they have taken the gospel once again this summer to Tibetan peoples. But their work is close to home, too, reaching the neglected elderly, the blind, and children with autism. I have been invited to see this work in action tomorrow.

**August 23, 2014**

Set out early this morning to meet up with Mei Li. We rendezvoused at Walmart and walked on for nearly a mile to one of the house church locations, where on Saturday mornings the Morning Light Club meets. This is a support group for autistic children and their parents that Mei Li and the Left Hand team started. Volunteers teach the children skills and give them opportunities to interact with the other children. The kids played a game, learned a song, then practiced their memory verse: "For by grace you have been saved through faith. And this is not your own doing; it is the gift of God, not a result of works, so that no one may boast" (Eph. 2:8–9).

But the main focus of today's session was to give the parents a chance to share their stories and struggles. In some ways, I think the parents suffer more than the children do. In this shame-based society, there is no real place for these children in the school system. The parents, like their kids, feel isolated, frustrated, and they suffer in silence. But the gospel shows us how broken we *all* are, just like the memory verse—no boasting, except in Jesus. So these moms and dads can open up to each other; and several, who have come to faith, are glorifying God through this trial, for they have never before experienced such unconditional love.

I noticed Mei Li holding the baby of one of the volunteers so the mom could participate with less distraction. My friend obviously enjoys seeing the medicine of love work on broken hearts. Mei Li is Jesus's hands to these parents and these little ones. Jesus said, "Let the little children come to me" (Matt. 19:14). At Morning Light, they and their moms and dads are doing just that. His grace, his embrace, also includes those who don't fit in.

This afternoon I tagged along with Mei Li as she checked in on another one of her bookstores in this city. She was especially eager to see the progress of her newest employee there. Wang Xu is eighteen years old and is going blind. She can see forms, but her condition is slowly worsening. In China, being a masseuse is about the only job prospect for a blind woman, and like her mother (who is also blind), Wang Xu was training for this work. But Mei Li knows the sexual abuse women in this profession are often subjected to, and so she hired Wang Xu to get her out of that bad situation.

Today, Wang Xu graduated from odd jobs at the store to working at the coffee bar—and she did very well. Mei Li was proud of her newest barista, and you could see the joy in Wang Xu's face, too, because someone loved her enough to take her, teach her, and give her a chance. And—best of all—someone loved her enough to tell her about Jesus, whom she has embraced in new life!

Both at Morning Light and at my sister Wang Xu's little celebration, I haven't met any experts. The Christians here aren't experts in helping autistic children, or counseling their parents, or in vocational training for the blind; but a person who is drowning can't wait for a boat to be built to save him. These believers are just diving in, knowing that while they don't have all the answers, they do have the ultimate answer—it's the radical rescue work of the gospel!

### Sunday, August 24, 2014

Met for worship this morning with about forty believers in a house church that meets in an upper room on the back side of a restaurant, through a door marked by a simple paper cross. Before they went to prayer, they sang songs to prepare their hearts: "'Tis so sweet to trust in Jesus" and "What can wash away my sins? Nothing but the blood of Jesus." Just as they sang in chorus, they prayed in chorus. They prayed for blessing, for help in the Word—and they prayed that the police would not come today. Recently they had been broken up by the police and had to regroup, so this was no idle prayer.

In this city where the crackdown on house churches has been more frequent, it's rare for foreigners to be included in these gatherings, but the pastor (who has taken the Christian name Jonah) has known me for many years so he welcomed me. And the people were welcoming, too. A sister gave me a Chinese-English Bible so I could join in the service better. Jonah opened his message from Luke 9, where Jesus said, "Leave the dead to bury their own dead. But as for you, go and proclaim the kingdom of God" (v. 60). It was very interactive as they followed the Word together. Pastor Jonah nearly drank himself blind before his conversion; so now when he reads the Scripture, he holds it to his face, squinting behind thick glasses. But Jonah has seen wonders of grace in it—and eagerly shares what he finds!

This gathering is just a microcosm of what is happening all over China this Lord's Day. Statistics are easy to come up with—but hard to verify—yet, even the most conservative sources put the number of Christians in China somewhere between sixty and eighty million. That means there are hundreds of thousands of house church meetings every Sunday in China!

After the message, we had the privilege of sharing the Lord's Table together. As Pastor Jonah broke unleavened bread, the people sang in a beautiful chant a song called, "Break the Bread of Life." Before we received the wine, they sang in chorus, "Raise the Cup of Salvation." Their songs of the cross and of the Lamb wafted out of open windows and mixed with the clamor of the busy street below.

Finished out the day at Mei Li's place. For security reasons, we had worshiped in different locations this Lord's Day. And so we traded stories of our day over dinner. Afterwards, Mei Li ground some rich Colombian coffee and made pour-overs. It was a perfect finish to a perfect day and a good time to catch our breath before our last homestretch of travel. Tomorrow we head westward to Inner Mongolia, where Mei Li has opened another Christian bookstore as a beachhead of gospel work in the region. We mapped out our plans for the journey, and remembered all the ways the Lord has gone before us all our days here—and we're eager to follow him tomorrow!

## Somewhere West of Xanadu, Inner Mongolia
### *August 27, 2014*

Early yesterday morning Mei Li and I caught a cab for the airport for our flight to Inner Mongolia. It was a perfect day for flying, and it felt like freedom to escape the high-rise megacity for the tableland of the interior. Inner Mongolia is a vast province of grasslands and Gobi sand and, of course, ever-growing cities.

Within China, it is the homeland of the descendants of Genghis Khan and his horsemen. The Mongol Empire once stretched from the Pacific to Poland, but a lot has changed since those glory days seven hundred to eight hundred years ago. Beijing has made a long-standing effort to keep control of its ethnic minorities on the fringes of the empire by resettling the majority Han people in those far-flung areas. The Mongolians in the region that bears their name are now a minority outnumbered five to one by the Han. Understandably, the Mongolians cling tenaciously to their culture, clans, language, and religion—a mixture of animism and Buddhism. Mei Li believes that if Mongolia is going to be reached with the gospel—penetrating its barriers and vastness—it will be done by Mongolians. So she has been discipling a team of Mongolians to be a gospel force here.

Reached Baotou late morning. A Mongolian sister named Chakha met us at the airport. She and Mei Li are definitely kindred spirits. Their friendship began seven years ago, when Chakha was a college student. At the time, Chakha was "fresh from the farm" and a thousand miles from home—new to the city, new to the faith. People in the church, unfortunately, were not welcoming to this shy, awkward college student. Chakha told me that part of the reason she kept to herself is because she didn't speak good Chinese—Mongolian was her first language. I think Mei Li understands lonely people better than most and is always looking for the one left out. She saw something in Chakha—not just someone she could disciple but someone who could reach her own people with the gospel.

Mei Li is an entrepreneurial disciple-maker. She sees an opportunity before there's anything to see—and then is willing to invest in the young disciple. Chakha now oversees the Christian bookstore that Mei Li started here—one of the first in the entire province of Inner Mongolia. We spent the afternoon at the bookshop, and Mei Li's mentoring was evident in the way Chakha cared for things and cared for people. The shop and café is in a university district, and several students were tucked into various nooks of the store tapping on laptops while tending cappuccinos. Chakha gave me a tour of the back and was delighted to show me their stock of Mongolian Bibles. Her language is written up and down in an elegant script that resembles a tangled fishing line.

Early evening, closed the shop and walked to supper. Chakha invited a woman to join us—someone I first noticed hanging out at the bookstore. I asked Mei Li who she was, and it turns out she is not a believer but is seeking. Her mother is in prison, and so she is an outcast, shunned by most everyone—except Chakha. It is so countercultural in China—and really in most places— to include an outsider in your group; but the gospel is countercultural. It is through witnesses like Chakha that the kingdom grows here—one by one, by the millions!

With Mei Li on the grasslands

Set out this morning for the grasslands with Mei Li, Chakha, and her friend Ghoa. Our road took us into a range called Daiqing—"The Great Green Mountains"—which opened up into the vast grasslands of Inner Mongolia. Marco Polo crossed these plains seven centuries ago and lived in the royal city of Xanadu, which now lies in ruins just to the east of us. Polo's journal with its stories of Xanadu's wealth and wonder ignited Europe's drive to explore—and the world was never the same.

This evening in the golden hour before sunset, took a walk with Mei Li. The sky was big, the grasslands seemed as if they would never end, and wildflowers dotted the expanse. As we walked, Mei Li told me of a turning point in her life out here under this sky. It was the year she started her first Christian bookstore, with all the real risks and hard realities involved. It was also the year her husband left her. It was the worst of times. She was invited to get away and come to a little Christian camp out on the grasslands. Her heart was filled with hurt and unanswered questions. God was unfair, and his love for her was little more than her mother's love—real, sure, but powerless to fix her problems. As her heart swirled with these hard questions, she wandered out into this vastness.

As night settled over the land and over her broken heart, she looked up. Mei Li was a city girl, so she had never seen such stars! The Milky Way—or what the Chinese call the Silver River—flooded the night with such light that the heavens seemed to nearly break beneath the weight of its glory. Mei Li was in utter awe—first of the stars, and then of the Maker of the stars. In that moment, a single word came to her mind as clearly as if God wrote it with his finger in starlight—*surrender*. She told me that night she was like Job. In the presence of her awesome God, she had no more questions, for he answered them all with just himself. This was Mei Li's place of surrender—a turning point in following Christ, reckless abandon beneath the stars. Since that night, she has faced threats, setbacks, and jail bars, but also open doors—gospel doors that no one can shut—as she walks in the bright wake of her Risen King.

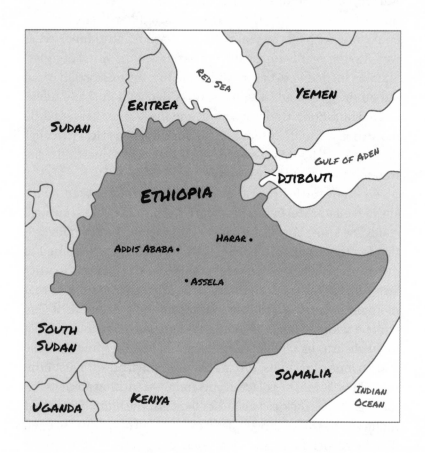

# 4

# Mercy. Multiplied.

## Michael Alemu (Ethiopia)

"If God should have no more mercy on us than we have charity to one another, what would become of us?"[1]
*Thomas Fuller*

If there were ever a passage of Scripture to put us in our place, it's Isaiah 55:8–9: "For my thoughts are not your thoughts, neither are your ways my ways, declares the LORD. For as the heavens are higher than the earth, so are my ways higher than your ways and my thoughts than your thoughts." This reality shatters our pretense and pride, but the setting of this passage does far more than remind us of how small we are because it is set in the midst of a stunning invitation in Isaiah 55:

> Come, everyone who thirsts,
>     come to the waters;
> and he who has no money,
>     come, buy and eat!

> Come, buy wine and milk
>> without money and without price.
> Why do you spend your money for that which is not bread,
>> and your labor for that which does not satisfy?
> Listen diligently to me, and eat what is good,
>> and delight yourselves in rich food.
> Incline your ear, and come to me;
>> hear, that your soul may live;
> and I will make with you an everlasting covenant,
>> my steadfast, sure love for David. . . .
> let the wicked forsake his way,
>> and the unrighteous man his thoughts;
> let him return to the LORD, that he may have compassion
>> on him,
>> and to our God, for he will abundantly pardon.
> For my thoughts are not your thoughts,
>> neither are your ways my ways, declares the LORD.
> For as the heavens are higher than the earth,
>> so are my ways higher than your ways
>> and my thoughts than your thoughts. (Isa. 55:1–3, 7–9)

Here in Isaiah, God's greatness and *difference* is displayed not by his ability to speak stars into existence, but by his mercy toward the least likely. God made a way for death-bound enemies to live and to be his sons and daughters and take their place at his table. As it is said, "Once you were not a people, but now you are God's people; once you had not received mercy, but now you have received mercy" (1 Pet. 2:10). The Scriptures are full of such sovereign surprises. One of the greatest examples of this is Paul. By transforming grace, Saul of Tarsus, the great persecutor of Christians, becomes Paul the Apostle, so that it was said, "'He who used to persecute us is now preaching the faith he once tried to destroy.' And they glorified God because of me" (Gal. 1:23–24). Surprising transformation is also the story of my friend Michael Alemu.

## Assela, Ethiopia
*March 5, 2011*

Drove from Harar to Assela today by making a long, dusty descent into the Great Rift Valley, the grand gash that cuts through the heart of Ethiopia. The poorly engineered and hastily paved road (courtesy of the lowest bidder) was as treacherous as my driver. Chinese contractors are building infrastructure and factories everywhere in exchange for access to Ethiopia's mineral wealth, but it seems this highway was a bad bargain. After some straight talk with the driver, we proceeded at a pace that at least kept all four tires on the road.

This asphalt strip snakes through country filled with color and wonder. The valley is a fertile, undulating floor between the cracked red faces of the wide Rift walls. Volcanic upheavals have scattered chunks of black-glass obsidian and red pumice on the surface and cut deep pools and waterfalls that supply the fields and attract a menagerie of bright birds. I saw iridescent blue flycatchers, green parrots, and black swans with wingtips dipped in snowy white. I also saw roving herds of camels, which gathered by the great pool south of Nazret, where they filled their backpacks with water before setting out on their desert march. This place is like a zoo without bars!

This evening finally reached Assela, where I'm staying with Michael Alemu. Michael is a gracious brother, graciousness that flows from grace. He ministers to orphans and broken people here in Assela and beyond. But Michael is also spearheading a number of efforts to evangelize the unreached in Ethiopia and to strengthen the church here through Word-centered, sustainable pastoral training. Michael is carrying on the work of ten men, yet he is unhurried and attentive.

After we scrubbed off the dust of the day, Michael hosted an Ethiopian coffee ceremony for me and his other guests. As we settled into some coffee, I asked Michael to tell me more of his story. Michael was born to a poor family in a poor village, but he got a chance to go to school, where he excelled. At seventeen, he was conscripted to fight in Ethiopia's war with Somalia. Those were the years of Mengistu, a tyrant who overthrew the monarchy, murdered the king, and, backed by Soviet arms, ruled with an iron fist. Michael quickly proved himself in the back-to-back wars with Somalia and Eritrea. Fighting was brutal, merciless, and personal, as all sides took revenge for atrocities committed. Like all men I've known who have seen real combat, Michael said little more than that the memories of the war are ones he has learned to keep in.

Michael Alemu

Michael's leadership under fire on the front lines got the attention of his superiors. As a proven soldier and devout Communist, Michael was selected to be part of a small, elite group sent to the Soviet Union to learn how to spread the doctrines of Marxism in order to bolster Mengistu's hold over the Ethiopian people. A starry-eyed Michael arrived in Moscow expecting to find the Communist utopia he had long heard of. Instead what he saw was a great gap between the Communist elites and their subjects, who were standing in long bread lines. The revolution's promise of liberation was just more slavery—a big shining lie. Michael returned to Ethiopia as a rising star to carry Communism to the masses, but in his heart he was deeply disillusioned—and things were about to get worse.

At that time, Ethiopia descended into what became known as the Red Terror, when Mengistu, in the paranoia of power, purged every threat, real or imagined. Tens of thousands of Ethiopians, mostly young people, were murdered gangland style over a period of a year. Every morning Michael walked past fresh corpses, and his sense of justice was shattered. Michael told me he saw murdered children and grieved that their families could not even recover their bodies for burial without paying a so-called "wasted bullet tax" to the thugs who had murdered them. Besides all that he saw, Michael himself was ordered to do things his conscience wouldn't allow. He told me that during this crisis of conscience, he remembered that when he was a child, every day before he set off for school in his little village, his mom would pluck a few sprigs of green grass and place them in his open hands and say, "Never do harm with these hands." All the crowded years of war and power and bloodshed could not silence his mother's plea: "Never do harm with these hands."

So, Michael joined a plot that was quietly taking shape to overthrow Mengistu and stop the killing. When the plot became known, most of the officers involved were executed; but Michael escaped. For three months he made his way across the forbidding terrain of southern Ethiopia, narrowly escaping death time and time again—from Mengistu's men, from lions, and from hunger. Eventually he made it across the border to Kenya. At the age of twenty-one, he found himself living on the streets of Nairobi as a homeless, nameless refugee.

After several months he met a pastor, who was not repulsed by his filthy condition. The pastor gave him not only a meal but the gospel, too—and Michael believed! Michael said his entire worldview was dismantled that day, as this pastor, who had everything in comparison to him, lowered himself, showed love and compassion (even embraced him in his filth and stench), and pointed him to Jesus, whose grace could save him to the uttermost. Not only was Michael born again, but he also knew what he wanted to do: "I want to be like this man." And so he did, by an amazing, winding path filled with sovereign surprises.

Michael eventually found refuge in Canada, met his wife, and started a family. He wasn't able to return to Ethiopia for many years until after Mengistu fell from power in 1991. When he was finally able to come back, he found that the Red Terror had left a million orphans. One evening as Michael was out walking, he heard a pleading voice, "Father, give me bread." It was a little orphan boy, perhaps five years old, one of the thousands living on the streets of Addis at the time. Somehow this particular child captured his heart. He gave him some money for food and asked him to come back in the morning.

That night Michael couldn't sleep. He lay in his bed and thought of that child sleeping on the street. Early in the morning he went out searching for the boy, but he couldn't find him. He searched the next day, too, but he never saw the boy again. I think the voice of that child still haunts him—and it changed his life and the lives of the hundreds of orphans Michael has rescued and raised over the past twenty years. Michael didn't set out to oversee the care, feeding, and education of hundreds of orphans. He simply answered the plea of a hungry, homeless child, and God opened his heart and his hands wider and wider. Tomorrow I will see more of the work, but for now, I sleep.

### March 6, 2011

I was not prepared for all I saw and heard today at the orphanage and school Michael started. The quality of the care, the extent of the work, and the sound of the children all gave me much joy! Over the past twenty years Michael and his team have raised over 2,500 orphans. Beyond that, they have provided educational opportunities in the public school system for children with special needs of all kinds: blind, deaf, and children with Down syndrome and autism. Tens of thousands are getting an education and hope for a future—children who otherwise would be outcasts.

Yerus

Michael has a special compassion for the children nobody wants. That's why he takes in orphans with AIDS. He took me over to meet them. Two little girls met us at the gate—Yerus and her friend Lamrot. Yerus, which is short for "Jerusalem," came here when she was four. Michael found her at the hospital—an orphan with full-blown AIDS, waiting to die. She had lost her hair, and her head was covered with sores instead. Michael made a little kerchief for her and took her out shopping for clothes. Afterwards, he determined he had to help her. Because she was the first child with AIDS that he had ever taken into the orphanage, his heart was filled with fear and uncertainty. Still though, two things were certain: left alone, Yerus would soon die; and Michael had to do something. So Yerus would be the beginning of taking care of AIDS orphans. Four years later, she has beautiful hair, which she had pulled back in a ponytail, and she has a strong faith and love for Jesus. There were seven other AIDS orphans at the orphanage when I visited. Michael said the children are the best therapy for each other—they take care of each other.

They all have their stories, which Michael shared as we watched them on the playground. Lamrot was one year old and her brother Nathaniel just four when their mother died, and Nathaniel took care of Lamrot until Michael learned of their plight and brought them here. Tamrat was found at the breast of his dead mother, who had died two days earlier. Tamrat's name means "miracle," but it seemed to me that there were eight miracles swirling around the yard—miracles of what gospel-driven love can do, miracles like Yerus, the little girl full of sores and left for dead now showing off her ponytail and winning my heart with her smile.

Michael wants to do more than simply meet needs. He wants to develop those with needs so that they can help themselves—and help others. It's the multiplication of mercy. I got a glimpse of how he's doing that when we went from the orphanage to other parts of the ministry scattered around Assela. Besides the various homes where the children and their caregivers live, there's a dairy farm, brick kiln, welding shop, and woodshop.

Visited the woodshop where men have been trained as furniture makers. Rough-hewn logs were being planed into boards, while finishing work was underway in other parts of the shop. Several of the men are deaf. Michael says "disability" does not mean "inability." With training and a chance, these men are supporting themselves and the ministry here. But Michael is also pushing them to improve. I think Michael is a bit like me—he probably can't build a birdhouse—but he knows excellence and he encourages the men so that the creations of their hands reflect their Creator. These brothers of mine give testimony to the One who loved the deaf. On the wall of their shop they have written the question: "Who is like our God?" It's a beautiful boast drawn from the Psalms, a passage whose truth these men know well: "Who is like the LORD our God? . . . He raises the poor from the dust and lifts the needy from the ash heap" (Ps. 113:5, 7).

Afterwards I asked if I could meet Tariku. A few months back I heard about this eleven-year-old boy's remarkable rescue story. No one knows who his father or mother are. He lived in the open like an animal—quite literally. The people in his town said he was smart, a survivor, because at night he slept with the wild dogs as protection from the hyenas. When Michael heard about the boy, he went and found him. The sight and smell of a boy who had never bathed didn't turn him away—just the opposite. He took him in, loved him, clothed him, and named him. Today when I visited, Tariku was working on his first-grade math homework, and we chatted a bit to practice his English. Then he showed me his room where he bunks with two other orphan boys. Even now it makes me tear up to think about it. Tariku sat on his bed, the only bed he has ever known. Less than a year ago, he was sleeping on the ground with the dogs. It was precious and humbling to see such grace on display. Michael is Jesus's hands to these outcasts, the unwashed and unwanted.

## Lake Ziway, Central Ethiopia
### March 9, 2011

Blue mist hangs over Lake Ziway as thick as the legends that still linger over these waters. An old tradition says that when Muslims invaded and conquered Ethiopia centuries ago, some Christians fled deep into the Great Rift Valley with the ark of the covenant. There they found refuge and hid their sacred treasure on an island in the middle of this lake. This evening, I took a leaky rowboat out on Ziway. I didn't see the ark, but I did see several hippopotamuses keeping watch along the shore. Myth or not, these days Christians are not retreating but advancing— dramatically and numerically.

I've had a front-row seat to the gospel breakthrough here in Oromo country. The Oromo are the largest people group in Ethiopia, numbering over thirty million and spread from the bor- der of Somalia through central and south Ethiopia and down into northern Kenya. They are predominantly Muslim, but Christ has set his love on these people. He has raised up men and women transformed and driven by the gospel, to take good news to their people, and there has been rapid advance of the kingdom among them. There are now about seven million Oromo believers—and one of them is my friend Michael. He has a great burden that his people would have the Bible in their heart language. There is an Oromo Bible, and there is a high literacy rate among the Oromo people, but the problem is supply. Michael estimates that only 2 percent of Oromo believers have the Scriptures in their language. With great effort he was able to secure a few boxes of Oromo New Testaments, and we set out today to make the first delivery to the village of Bosha.

Reached Bosha, where amid a scattering of huts was a simple mud-daubed church building, where we gathered with Christians in worship. Just one year ago, the leader of this band of believers was the sheikh in this Muslim village. Sheikh Jaru's two sons, Abdullah and Muzemir, had become Christians—and for this, their father beat them with a horse whip and kicked them out. Hungry and penniless, they walked forty miles to Assela where they found a pastor who fed them—and then took them back to Bosha to face the sheikh. The pastor appealed to Jaru, father to father, and he also shared Christ with him. Jaru said he would read the Bible and decide for himself what was true. In the Scripture he saw Jesus Christ—*Isa Masih*—and believed on him. After Jaru's conversion (or, as he puts it, "when I became a new person"), he went to the mosque and proclaimed Christ. What came next was like reading Acts 9. After Saul's conversion, "immediately he proclaimed Jesus in the synagogues, saying, 'He is the Son of God.' And all who heard him were amazed and said, 'Is not this the man who made havoc in Jerusalem of those who called upon his name?'" (Acts 9:20–21). Just as Saul went to the synagogues, Sheikh Jaru went to the mosques in the area and boldly proclaimed Christ. He also gave his property for a church meeting place, and more and more are turning from darkness to light.

However, such gospel advance is being met with violence. Reports have come in that west of here in Jimma, one Christian was killed by a Muslim mob, several were wounded with machetes, and nearly fifty churches and Christians' homes were burned down. The trigger for this violence is the fact that Islam is losing ground in that district. Thousands of Muslims, including imams, have become Christians. I'm told some of their meeting places used to be mosques. But no amount of building-burning or machete-slashing can stop our King! It's really out of their hands. They do not yet know the power of the gospel or the One who said in Isaiah, "I work, and who can turn it back?" (43:13).

God's unstoppable work was evident here today. The box of Oromo Bibles was distributed, followed by a time of prayer and praise. They sang of the power of Jesus to save and for the blessing of receiving his Word for the first time—to read and to hear Jesus speak Oromo. Their worship was lively, but why not? They've seen the iron bars of Islam snapped like a stick. They were dead but have now been raised up by the living Christ. As Isaiah said, "Behold, your God . . . He will come and save you. . . . The eyes of the blind shall be opened, and the ears of the deaf unstopped; then shall the lame man leap like a deer, and the tongue of the mute sing for joy" (Isa. 35:4–6).

Michael wants this joy to spread far and wide among the Oromo people from here southward to Kenya and eastward to Somalia. But without a Bible in their heart language, this can't happen. This need for Oromo Bibles is much on his mind. He told me, "Recently, I gave ten Oromo Bibles to an evangelist in central Ethiopia. He was joyful in receiving them, but he turned around and said, 'I have twenty missionaries who are ready to go. To which of these twenty am I going to give these ten Bibles?'

Imagine a church with only one Bible for the entire congregation. That is the situation we are in today."

Getting the Word out: Oromo Bible distribution

For Michael, ever the man of action, seeing churches without Bibles was unacceptable. So within a year after the conversation I had with him about the growing need for Oromo Bibles, Michael was overseeing the distribution of a ship container of sixty thousand Oromo Bibles! He gathered partners in Ethiopia, Canada, and the United States to fund the Bibles. He also organized the most critical, difficult, and often overlooked component of such a large-scale project: distribution, actually putting the Bibles into the hands of Oromo Christians. Michael and his team, who had a history of meeting needs, distributing care, and implementing programs, had the experience and integrity to do the job. The Bibles were given out church by church until the last box was emptied, whether a church was in a city or one that could be reached only by foot. This first ship container was not the last. Over the next five years, over half a million Oromo Bibles and New Testaments were distributed. These Bibles were nation-shaking in strengthening the church and advancing the gospel, even in the hardest places where Islam has long held sway. Five years after the Bible project started, I caught up with Michael in his home in Assela.

## Assela, Ethiopia
### December 15, 2017

It seemed that Christmas came early. I had so much fun today talking over the many miles and years that have passed between Michael and me. My friend is a bit grayer now, but his joy and the joy he gives are greater than ever. And his energy seems undiminished. He'll need this energy, because at age sixty-one, with his children grown and on their own, Michael and his wife have adopted two boys from the orphanage. Daniel and Zakariah were just coming in from school—when I was last here they were just toddlers at the orphanage. Both were abandoned at birth—Zakariah at a hospital and Daniel on the bank of a river. They are home now, and Michael is a proud "new" dad again.

I asked about Tariku and Yerus, the rescued children I met years ago. Tariku is in ninth grade now—a bright, industrious student and at a point where he is now thinking about what he wants to do with his life. Perhaps one day he will take the place of the man who first loved him. Yerus, the AIDS orphan I last watched on a swing set, is a young lady now—a seventh grader who has been adopted and who Michael says loves to sing—and loves Jesus! Apart from Michael's risk-taking love, Yerus would have been in an unmarked grave years ago. Now she is growing, learning, singing, and glorifying the God of grace!

Our conversation felt like I was drinking from a fire hydrant. The number of Oromo Bibles Michael and his team have distributed is now at half a million. Michael said putting the Bible in the language and hands of Oromo Christians has been the "greatest fulfillment of my life and one that will impact generations to follow." It has been like planting a strong tree. The roots of the church here are deepening through Word-centered preaching, and in a surprising result, literacy rates are rising within the churches as literate Oromo people teach illiterate ones so that they can read the Bible for themselves.

While the roots are deepening, the branches are growing, stretching, and pushing out into new territory. Michael said that almost every week twenty to thirty Muslim-background believers are being baptized, and many of them are former imams and sheikhs who are now preaching Christ and willing to die for him. The gates of hell are giving way, and life is coming out of hard ground! As Isaiah said,

> For as the rain and the snow come down from heaven
>     and do not return there but water the earth,
> making it bring forth and sprout,
>     giving seed to the sower and bread to the eater,
> so shall my word be that goes out from my mouth;
>     it shall not return to me empty,
> but it shall accomplish that which I purpose,
>     and shall succeed in the thing for which I sent it.
> For you shall go out in joy
>     and be led forth in peace;
> the mountains and the hills before you
>     shall break forth into singing,
>     and all the trees of the field shall clap their hands.
>         (Isa. 55:10–12)

Today I heard notes of this song on the hills around Assela as they echoed our stories of grace and the laughter of children once left for dead.

# A Hero in the Battle of Life

## Carl Keesee (Danville, Virginia)

"The silver thread of resurrection runs through all the believer's blessings, from his regeneration onwards to his eternal glory, and binds them together."[1]

*Charles Spurgeon*

Among my many books is a slim volume stamped in gold. It's a nineteenth-century gospel tract, a common story crowned with uncommon faith and sacrifice, titled *A Hero in the Battle of Life*. Over the years, I have known a few men who fit that description. One of them was my father.

### Antalya, Turkey
*February 28, 2013*

Before leaving Azerbaijan for Turkey yesterday, I received word that hospice care had been called in for Daddy. I was finally able to get a call out to him late tonight and found a long, lonely stretch of Mediterranean beach where we talked for a few minutes. He could hear the crashing of the waves and asked where I was and when I was coming home. I described the sea and the stars for him, but he was too weak to talk much, drifting in and out. And then the call was over. I tried so desperately to recall everything he said, until the memory of his voice and the sound of the sea seemed almost indistinguishable. I'm afraid I will forget the sound of his voice. I don't know how long I stood there. It was cold, and the tide crept up to my feet. The stars of Orion fell westward as the moon rose and followed them. As I stood beneath it all, I tried to remember what was said and what wasn't said, until the cold wind and the sickness of sorrow drove me back from the sea.

Carl Keesee

## Danville, Virginia
### *March 9, 2013*

The house is emptying. Memories are still here; in fact, they press upon me. But, like the room where Daddy died last Sunday, life is seeping out of this place. His books, the odd assortment of pocket knives on his dresser, clothes in his closet, the pictures on the wall—for now, nothing has moved, but something is missing.

I walked through Daddy's machine shop in the backyard. He was a skilled machinist and had a reputation for being able to fix anything—and he lived up to it. He repaired engines of all kinds—planes, trains, tractors, every sort of vehicle whether it had two wheels or four or eighteen. Once he even repaired a blimp that got stranded at the city airport. And because we live in a broken world, Daddy kept busy. But today the shop is quiet. The air smells of steel and grease. It's a good smell—smells like his hands.

Daddy's tools as he left them

A wrench lay on the workbench, where he left it. Over the past year, with his heart wearing out and vision and memory clouding, he slowly lost his grip on these tools, until he had to let them go altogether. But while Daddy's once-strong hands were losing their hold on things, Christ's hold on him never did. His last day on this side, while slipping in and out of consciousness, he began to sing to himself some songs my brother and sisters could not recognize. The one that was clear was "Amazing Grace."

When word reached me that he had died, I was on the other side of the world; but he was already well beyond all of us by then. I made it back for his funeral yesterday. The sun was brilliant against a sky so blue it hurt to look upon it. His grandsons, including my son, carried the flag-draped casket to its place— an open grave in the Virginia clay, like a fresh wound in the earth. On a hillside nearby, an honor guard fired three volleys above us, and the trumpet sounded "Taps"—it was clear, sweet, and sad. The next time a trumpet sounds over this grave, it will not be for a soldier, but for a saint. "For the Lord himself will descend from heaven with a cry of command, with the voice of an archangel, and with the sound of the trumpet of God. And the dead in Christ will rise first" (1 Thess. 4:16).

### March 10, 2013

This morning, I went back out to Daddy's grave. There were no long black cars, no funeral tent, no gun salutes or Taps. The flag is now folded and treasured. Blue birds flitted about the cemetery, and between the grave markers, violets and dandelions were pushing through the late winter ground. The wreath on his grave was still fresh. I sat there and wondered why I could not have made it back to see him once more and to finish the conversation we started by the sea, but I thought of a character in one of Daddy's favorite books. In *The Pilgrim's Progress*, the courageous, prayerful Mr. Standfast is journeying on and encouraging other pilgrims along the way, when suddenly a courier arrives from the Celestial City. He delivers a message to Mr. Standfast that explains "that he must prepare for a change of life, for his Master was not willing that he should be so far from him any longer."[2] Then I remembered a little note left in Daddy's papers in the room where he died. It was simply a Scripture reference: John

15:16. After calling his disciples "friends," Jesus said, "You did not choose me, but I chose you." And above it, Daddy had written one strong, certain, gracious word: *chosen*. And so, the risen Christ has called up his chosen one to be with him. No wonder Daddy sang of such amazing grace as he crossed the river—beyond this red clay portal, strewn with flowers.

## Artillery Road
### Sunday, June 15, 2013

It's the last of the last hour of daylight. The ancient oak next to my back porch here stretches his arms into the slanted golden light and shadow-boxes with the sun. The cardinal, dove, and thrush are saying good night, as their choir calls it a day. I've noticed there is a brief lull in the evening, like a short intermission at a concert. It's the shift change between the birds and the bugs, when the crickety, croaking night sounds fill the darkness and fireflies fan their fannies for another light show.

But for now the skylight is enough. The coffee is good, and I need to write. This Sunday, Father's Day, has been filled with reminders of God's grace in and through my father's life. Through the Savior, my Father's House is now my father's house; but not a day goes by that I do not think of him. I wish we could talk tonight.

Some things are still too close to write about, but I know Daddy would not want me sad today. He isn't—and for that reason alone (a reason rooted in the gospel), I need not be either. So I will remember with joy some of the things he taught me, the way his life shaped mine and still gives me an example to strive for.

Carl Keesee was the son of a sharecropper. He quit school after ninth grade. There was no future for him on the farm; so he went to work in a machine shop, where he demonstrated from the beginning his genius for all things mechanical. When he served in the Air Force, he traded car engines for jet engines and got to see more of the country than anyone in my family had seen since my ancestors marched on Gettysburg in 1863! Our roots run deep in the red clay of the Virginia foothills. Daddy would describe to me the adventures of being stationed in New York or Texas, but most of his stories were about hitchhiking home!

He and my mother raised five children of their own—and many more besides, as Mama babysat children at the house to help meet the bottom line. It was normal for Daddy to work up to sixty hours a week—first at the machine shop and then, after supper, repairing cars in our yard. An accident in the Air Force had left Daddy blind in one eye. I am not sure how he worked in the conditions he did with only one good eye, but I never heard him complain even once.

Some people say more than they do. Others do more than they say—Daddy was in that group. He was a man of few words, quiet, even shy in a crowd; for him, love and hard, sacrificial labor were bound up together. They were not separate, scheduled events. Growing up I don't recall that he went to any of my baseball games or track meets or band concerts. But he put his time in for me in other ways—often under someone's car with wrenches and ratchets and strong hands blackened with oil and grease. Even if he wasn't in the bleachers, he always seemed to be with me because I knew he loved me with steadfast love. He loved this way because God loved him that way, only more so—saving, lasting, unbroken love.

After he died, I found the last passage marked from his daily Bible reading. It was Psalm 86. I was amazed with joy to read Daddy's testimony echoing David's prayer:

Incline your ear, O LORD, and answer me,
    for I am poor and needy.
Preserve my life, for I am godly;
    save your servant, who trusts in you—you are my God.
Be gracious to me, O Lord,
    for to you do I cry all the day.
Gladden the soul of your servant,
    for to you, O Lord, do I lift up my soul.

For you, O Lord, are good and forgiving,
> abounding in steadfast love to all who call upon you.
> (Ps. 86:1–5)

A few weeks ago when I was back in Virginia, I noticed the grass has nearly finished covering Daddy's grave, healing that little patch of red clay. My heart, though, seems to be taking much longer to heal. But steadfast love steadies me tonight, for it is unshaken even by death—Jesus forever saw to that! Looking to him fills the empty places of this day. In the bright wake of the risen Christ, my sorrow is brushed away like tears.

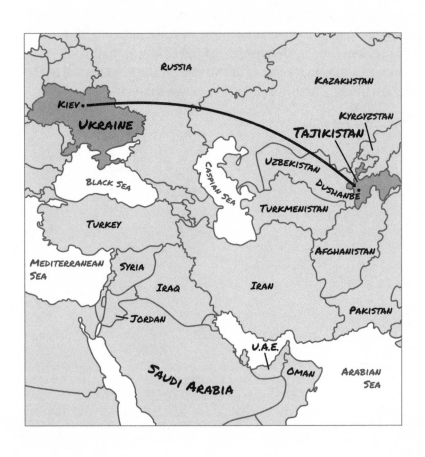

# 6

# Rise and Fight Again

## Ivan and Oksana (Central Asia)

"Not only that, but we rejoice in our sufferings, knowing that suffering produces endurance, and endurance produces character, and character produces hope, and hope does not put us to shame, because God's love has been poured into our hearts through the Holy Spirit who has been given to us." (Rom. 5:3–5)

"We have so often been disappointed that we must not be too sure of anything, save of God's help and presence which He will never withhold."[1]

*Hudson Taylor*

Recently a friend and I visited Washington's Crossing, Pennsylvania. That day the Delaware River was a perfect mirror reflecting a crisp blue-and-white sky—the silver glass waters rippled only by lolling, lazy geese shaking off a nap as we slipped down to the river's edge. Giant sycamores shade the bank where an old stone marker reads:

> Near this spot Washington
> Crossed the Delaware
> On Christmas night 1776
> The eve of the Battle of Trenton

There could hardly have been a more striking contrast between that peaceful afternoon and the desperate, dangerous night when Washington risked everything.

Crossing the Delaware was a bold turn at the end of a long retreat. The fall of '76 had been a season of setbacks. Outnumbered and outgunned, many of Washington's soldiers had little to show for their service but their gaunt frames and a knack for digging graves. At the end of the year, just days away, their enlistments would expire, and in all of the war there was hardly a more critical time, as the destiny of a nation wavered on the edge of a knife. For Washington, the greatest risk was not taking one; so on Christmas Day, in the teeth of a storm, he crossed the river here and captured an enemy that was celebrating too soon. Trenton was a desperate victory that would prove Washington's daring, but it was only a respite. The following December, after another year of defeats and retreats, Washington's army made their way out of New York to winter quarters in the Pennsylvania countryside. They had little food and little hope. Washington grimly observed that "you might have tracked the army from White Marsh to Valley Forge by the blood of their feet."[2] The resilience of this unlikely army is all the more extraordinary considering that there were yet four more years of war ahead of them. One of Washington's generals, Nathanael Greene, would remark on their uneven path to final victory: "We fight, get beat, rise, and fight again."[3]

I have often thought of Greene's words in connection with the gospel's global advance, especially when pressing into the least-reached areas. It should not surprise us that the difficult places are, in fact, difficult and that for Christians in many regions of the world, suffering is as much a part of their faith as comfort is a part of ours. That's been true of Ivan and Oksana, who, early on in their marriage and ministry, were severely tested. God gave them tenacious grace to rise and fight again. And again. I caught up with them in Central Asia, three thousand miles from their native Ukraine to hear their story firsthand.

## Kiev, Ukraine
### February 5, 2017

It's early Sunday morning, and whether or not the sun is up can be determined only by the clock. The sky hangs heavy over Kiev, capping the tops of the canyons of cold, concrete high-rises that crowd roads paved with gray ice and lined with grubby gray mounds of snow.

A day and night of flying got me here just long enough to catch a few hours of sleep and a red-eye shot of espresso before heading out for another day-and-night flight further east to Tajikistan on the icy fringes of the old Soviet Empire.

## Dushanbe, Tajikistan
### February 6, 2017

On our approach to Dushanbe at dawn, the rugged Pamir Range looked like an arctic ocean, a frozen vastness of ice and stone. On the ground, the city was swirling with fog and flurries, and the temperature hung just north of zero. Ivan and Oksana were waiting outside the airport and welcomed me warmly, and they had a surprise for me—Timur is here from Uzbekistan. I haven't seen this brother in nearly ten years! Timur was a great mentor to Ivan when he and Oksana served in Uzbekistan. Their friendship didn't grow out of long chats in pleasant places, but was forged in a jail cell as they were handcuffed together for the sake of the gospel. Timur taught Ivan how to stand for Christ even while being struck to the floor by fists and clubs.

With Timur in Dushanbe

Went on to Ivan and Oksana's apartment for breakfast and some strong black tea to shake off the jet lag and the cold. It was good to see their children and hear how they are settling into a new country after just a few months. They had been ministering in the nearby police state of Uzbekistan for five years—sharing the gospel, planting a house church, making disciples primarily among Muslim people. They were effective in loving people to Jesus, but they were also attracting the attention of officials and felt they were close to being deported. Rather than be deported and blacklisted so they couldn't return, they packed up and moved next door to another Muslim country.

I love to see their love—how they love Jesus, love each other, and love others. They had such an impact for the gospel in Uzbekistan, and they are already at it again here in Tajikistan by sharing their faith in the market, starting Bible studies, opening their home. The kind of outreach Ivan saw modeled at his church growing up was inviting or convincing people to join the group, but what he and his wife learned and now live out is, in his words, that "evangelism is inviting people to join your family rather than inviting people to join your organization."

There was so much more to talk over, especially with Timur here, but I've been awake for most of the past three days, and sleep beckons with a persuasive hand.

### February 9, 2017

I am up, but the sun is not. From my window I can see traffic lights that, like me, stupidly stare and blink at empty, snow-lined streets. I can't sleep; so I'll write. My days have been too packed with motion and meetings to write; so this is a good time to catch up.

Had a good, long conversation yesterday with Ivan, Oksana, and Timur. Having the three of them together was a unique opportunity made possible because last week when Timur traveled from Uzbekistan by bus to visit his friends, his passport was stolen at the Dushanbe station. He now awaits the creaky gears of bureaucracy to turn and churn out a new passport so he can return home. I'm sorry for his predicament—the frustration and delay in getting back to his family—but at the same time we all agreed that God has given us a gift of these days together!

Ten years ago something important happened that I've long wanted to hear more about firsthand. From the outset of their marriage, Ivan and Oksana had a desire to serve Christ beyond the borders of their native Ukraine and take the good news to those who have yet to hear it. They met Timur in Ukraine when he was there to share his testimony of transforming grace in some churches. Timur was a Muslim and adamantly opposed to Christianity until he saw the change in his brother Ansur's life when he came to Christ. The change was undeniable, and his faith stood strong even in the rejection and violent opposition of his family. Through the power of the gospel, Timur and Ansur became twice-born brothers!

Ivan and Oksana

Timur invited Ivan to come to Uzbekistan to learn and to help out with an "underground" Christian camp Timur was overseeing. So Ivan went. He and Oksana had a newborn at the time; so she stayed behind. It was Ivan's first time out of the country, and within a week he was with Timur in a remote area of the country, where they had rented an old "Soviet Pioneers" Communist youth facility to hold a camp for Christian families. About thirty people came—many of them, like Timur, were Muslim-background believers, so the time of fellowship in the Word and with each other was precious. On the third night, as Timur was teaching from 1 Timothy—his Bible in one hand and his infant daughter in his other arm—they were raided by heavily armed, uniformed and plain-clothes police, with some even carrying submachine guns.

Ivan said his heart and mind swirled with fears and questions. "What will I do? What should I say—or not say?" But then he steadied his heart. In the chaos, cursing, and shouting that suddenly fell upon them, he said to himself, "I need to pray first and trust the Lord."

What followed for Ivan, Timur, and the other men there was a night of interrogations, humiliations, and beatings—mostly with rubber sticks, which are better for bruising rather than breaking the skin. Timur and Ivan jokingly called this "getting a massage." For the next several days, Timur and Ivan shared a jail cell and were handcuffed together. They said, "We had lots of time to get to know each other." Like Paul and Silas long ago in a Philippian jail, they, too, sang hymns of praise from their cell. In Uzbek they sang:

> You are my God.
> You are more precious than silver or gold.
> You are my hope, and my trust.

The other Christians also stood firm through these hard days and nights in the face of torture. Their assailants used police gas masks to suffocate them while beating them with rubber sticks and putting their feet in acid. Timur said of several new Christians among them, who had recently turned from Islam, "They went through the fire and came out on fire for the Lord." One of the brothers was Aziz. He was a big, strong man, a former wrestler who had served in the army. He could withstand the physical blows better than the rest of them, but there was a spiritual fight going on in his heart. The police wanted to humiliate him, and so they brought in a thirteen-year-old boy from the kids in the camp and told Aziz to get down and kiss the boy's feet, an act of great shame in that culture. But Aziz thought to himself, "If Jesus could wash his disciples' feet, then I can kiss the feet of my little brother." And so Aziz got down and kissed the boy's feet. The police roared in laughter and mocked him; but Aziz overcame his pride, identified with Christ, and made a long stride in running after his cross-bearer who, too, endured the derision, the slaps, and spit of his tormentors. Timur said it looked like the police had won a great victory, but actually Aziz won something far greater—joy in the fellowship of Christ's sufferings.

Another brother, Hamid, had only recently come to faith out of Islam. Being from the Muslim stronghold of the Ferghana Valley, the police beat him mercilessly and drove needles under his fingernails in an effort to get him to reject Christ. But he would not. Through tears of pain he said, "I will not deny Christ. I've seen his power in my life. I cannot deny Christ." Watching all this unfold, Ivan said seeing Hamid's courage gave him courage that night.

One of the interesting details of the night of the raid was that when they were first taken, the men were all searched, and their cell phones, wallets, and identification cards were taken. But somehow the policeman had missed Ivan's cell phone. During the interrogation, Ivan held the phone under the table and typed this text to his wife back in Ukraine: "They took us and won't let us go." When he hit "send," the phone buzzed to confirm delivery, and the interrogator heard it and took Ivan's phone.

I asked Oksana what she did when she got Ivan's text. She said, "It was after almost midnight in Kiev; so I prayed and went to sleep." She added that she doesn't usually panic and knew she had a baby to care for; so she simply prayed and went to bed. The next day she reached out to government officials to press for her husband's release. One person told her, "They will likely be kept long enough for the bruises to heal to cover up the police's work." And so it was. After a week, they were all released—and Ivan was put on a plane for Kiev.

For much of the next five years, Ivan and Oksana lived in the Crimea region of Ukraine, where a wise pastor named Tahir shepherded their hearts. It was a time when they grew in their depth in the Word and their walk with God. Their family grew, too, as two more children came along. Tahir, a former Muslim, mentored them in how to love and lead Muslims to Christ. The Crimea is home to Tatars, a Muslim people group.

In the 1940s, Stalin had the Tatar people deported en masse in cattle cars from Crimea to Uzbekistan. Tens of thousands died on this trail of tears, and even more died in forced labor. The survivors settled in Uzbekistan, and it wasn't until the 1980s that the Soviet government began to allow Tatars to return to their native Crimea. Some went back, and some stayed.

As Ivan and Oksana began to share life and the gospel with their Tatar neighbors in Crimea, they learned that they all had relatives in Uzbekistan. These ties of the Tatar people also drew Ivan's heart back to the place he felt deeply drawn to. He said that one day while walking along a road the thought came to him, "I could go back to Uzbekistan. It's been five years, so the arrest record may be overlooked. I must definitely try."

Ivan shared his idea with Oksana. He said, "We will go as a family, and we will drive to Uzbekistan. Crossing the border with our children will lower suspicion. We will stay for three months, and then decide after that if we will make our home and ministry in Uzbekistan."

Oksana told me initially the idea sounded "interesting and adventurous," but when she considered the long drive with three children five and under, she was terrified. They would drive from Ukraine, across southern Russia, crossing the steppes and deserts of Kazakhstan, and then face the unknowns at the Uzbek border. According to Ivan's careful calculations and mapping, they could make it by driving from five in the morning until eleven at night five days in a row. Of course, there were three borders to cross, which meant three unknown variables in the timetable. Despite being daunted by the distance, Oksana jumped into the task with her usual spirit, and the two of them worked through all the logistics of their great trek. So the five of them set out on a journey that would indeed be "interesting and adventurous," as well as hard and hot and ultimately life-changing.

The first big challenge was at the Russian-Kazakh border, where they were told that they could not cross with their children. The police said, "Turn back!" They were halfway to Uzbekistan but had hit a wall. They spent the night with some local Christians in Astrakhan and talked to family and friends back in Ukraine. Their friends advised them to come back, too, and accept that sometimes God leads by closed doors. They said, "You have shown God that you were willing to go, and that's enough; so you should come home." But both Ivan and Oksana felt they should find a way forward. Early the next morning, Ivan said, "We began with eager prayers to find a way to go and praises to him for his omnipresent power." Then they met with a border official who was kind (a miracle in itself!). He said their documents were in good order and there was no reason for them not to proceed. "Go back to the border police and give them my name and number if they have questions." Wow! God took a closed door and nailed it open. Within an hour, they were on their way and into Kazakhstan.

They were also in a desert for the first time in their lives—with its vast barrenness, broken only by the sight of camels and scattered yurts and mud-brick houses. It had a strange, striking beauty about it. But the wonder of it all came to halt at the Uzbek border. Trucks and cars were backed up for several miles because the border was closed. All day they sat waiting and sweltering on that desert road. The temperatures were about 115 degrees Fahrenheit. Finally during the night, the border opened again. When Ivan and his family got to the border station to get their documents checked and their vehicle searched, he told me the border police were very sleepy. Ivan actually had to wake up the one who was to inspect his documents, and the officer carelessly checked and stamped his documents and sent them on their way.

They were indeed on their way. It had been a five-year-long road since Ivan's arrest, but now he and his family were back in Central Asia, where they longed to "go and . . . speak to the people all the words of this Life" (Acts 5:20). The three-month visit would turn into five years of fruitful ministry.

Though Ivan and Oksana have now moved to yet another country, they are pilgrims who, like the desert-crossing Abraham before them, could "by faith . . . go out to a place that he was to receive as an inheritance. And he went out, not knowing where he was going" (Heb. 11:8). Abraham and Sarah and Ivan and Oksana could live and love and risk like this because they "considered him faithful who had promised" (Heb. 11:11).

The streets outside are brightening. The city is stirring. Time to go find coffee and then say farewell to my dear pilgrim-friends here at this cold, distant outpost of Christ's kingdom.

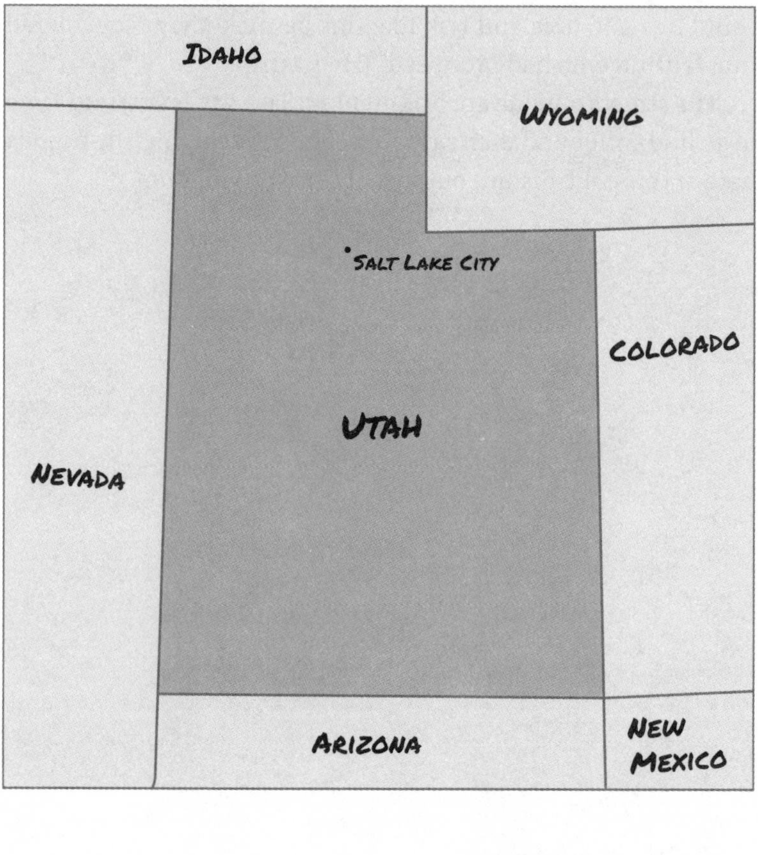
Idaho
Wyoming
Salt Lake City
Colorado
Utah
Nevada
Arizona
New Mexico

# 7

# Shepherds

## Danny Brooks (Salt Lake City, Utah)

"Remember your leaders, those who spoke to you the word of God. Consider the outcome of their way of life, and imitate their faith." (Heb. 13:7)

"Now, as they went up, Mr. Great-heart drew his Sword, with intent to make a Way for the Pilgrims."[1]

*John Bunyan*

When I was ten years old, my mother was recovering from an extended stay in the hospital and my father was working long hours to pay the bills and provide for four children—the oldest of us was eleven and the youngest was three. I will never forget the night our pastor, Paul Osborne, came to our house with groceries—and then took out some pots and pans and cooked our supper. He "preached" a sermon in our kitchen with his sleeves rolled up—hot biscuits, fried ham, and sweet tea were his sermon! The smell of good food mingled with the fragrance of Christ that night long ago.

It is significant that since the first century when congregations were springing up from Jerusalem to the frontiers of the empire and beyond, those responsible for the care, feeding, and protection of the churches were called shepherds. Pastors. Pastor is not so much a title as a responsibility and is directly tied to one of the ways God describes his relationship with his people. Peter, who was directed by the Good Shepherd himself to "feed my sheep," wrote:

> So I exhort the elders among you, as a fellow elder and a witness of the sufferings of Christ, as well as a partaker in the glory that is going to be revealed: shepherd the flock of God that is among you, exercising oversight, not under compulsion, but willingly, as God would have you; not for shameful gain, but eagerly; not domineering over those in your charge, but being examples to the flock. And when the chief Shepherd appears, you will receive the unfading crown of glory. (1 Pet. 5:1–4)

As these under-shepherds reflect the gospel-centered humility and Word-centered care of the Great and Good Shepherd, they bless his flock. I have been blessed over the years to know such shepherds. Pastor Osborne fed the little flock in my church from the Bible and from our kitchen. Other men also shepherded my soul by Word and by deed. In my teen years, W. L. Wade was my pastor. He was just twenty-six years old when he and his wife came to my church, but he was already a careful student and capable, passionate expositor of the Word. Under his preaching, I saw Christ in the Scriptures as never before. But Wade gave me something else—his time—whether on the basketball court or in conversations after church on Sunday nights. He also taught me to play chess, which I learned by losing repeatedly—*and* by not quitting. I lost sixty-seven games before I finally took his king!

Looking back now, I see that W. L. Wade was discipling me. Not through some best-selling plan but by preaching the Word on Sunday and living it out with consistency, wisdom, and winsomeness the rest of the week. In short, I wanted to love and serve Jesus more after being with my pastor who loved and served Jesus more.

Paul wrote to the Corinthians, "For though you have countless guides in Christ, you do not have many fathers" (1 Cor. 4:15). During my critical beginning years of ministry, my spiritual father was Pastor Frank Washburn. He was an eloquent pulpiteer, a man of intimate and forceful prayer—and he was always in motion! Washburn's influence was life-changing and ministry-shaping. Even after I married and moved away, a steady stream of letters from his pen always pointed me to Christ. Although he has been with the Lord now for many years, there is hardly a day that I don't think of him or hear echoes of his voice in mine. Here are my journal entries from the time of his homegoing.

Frank Washburn in 1990

113

## Artillery Road
### *June 30, 2002*

Frank Washburn's last words to me came in a little note a few days ago, which I reread tonight while I was sitting in my study:

Dear Tim,

I praise the Lord for helping you to lengthen your cords and strengthen your stakes. Isa. 54:2.

The whitened harvest fields are calling and so few are answering.

Hope to see you soon. Lamentations 3:26, "It is good that a man should both hope and quietly wait for the salvation of the LORD."

Frank E. Washburn

This Lord's Day morning his waiting ended. At daybreak he must have heard an invitation like Martha of Bethany once whispered: "The Master is come, and calleth for thee" (KJV). Yet tonight the heart that beat for God and the hands that pointed so many to the Savior are still. I feel a deep sense of loss—not just personally, but also in the gospel cause. For over sixty years he faithfully preached the Word, shepherded flocks, and encouraged young preachers. He was one of the greatest influences on my ministry. The Bible says God sought for a man to stand in the gap. Mr. Washburn was that man for me.

I recall how, when I was fifteen and called to preach, he invited me to preach at his church on a Sunday morning—my first Sunday service. I remember how he and his deacons sat there, leaning forward, listening intently, as if the Apostle Paul were filling in that morning. They did not have to listen long, for what the sermon lacked in content and coherence, it also lacked in length . . . a week of sermon preparation somehow shrank into seven minutes! For years afterward people recalled it as the day everyone got Sunday dinner early.

Despite that feeble start, Mr. Washburn had me back in the pulpit again that night. It wasn't that he recognized some great talent—it was that he understood what God's grace could do in a surrendered life, and so he was careful not to break a bruised reed.

Throughout high school and college, disappointments and triumphs, he was always there. Tonight his oft-repeated words steady me. When I was tempted to quit school and go out and preach, he said, "You can't cut down a tree with a dull axe. Keep your axe sharp, and the Lord will give you work." "Live for immortal things," he would say. When I needed counsel and comfort, he would say, "I'll be on my knees for you," and the prayers that followed always caused me to look to Christ and not myself. Tonight I can hear him so clearly say:

> The thorns in my path are not sharper
> Than composed His crown for me.
> The cup that I drink not more bitter
> Than He drank at Gethsemane.[2]

Those heart-to-heart conversations he had with God became face-to-face this morning.

### Martinsville, Virginia
*July 3, 2002*

Mr. Washburn's funeral was held this afternoon. The cemetery was on a ridge covered with old oaks and lichened marble. Beyond, the Blue Ridge Mountains crowned the horizon—fading into the haze of this hot July day.

The strange thing was that as soon as the casket was removed from the hearse, the skies darkened and suddenly opened up. We followed the pallbearers down the slippery hill to the grave. By then the rain had turned into a torrent, and we all huddled beneath the funeral tent. Bright twisted ribbons of lightning spun down and crackled in the trees above us. W. L. read Scripture, and

I had the final prayer; but our voices were nearly drowned out by the cascade above us.

Afterwards, I stood for a while on the ridge in the downpour. Drenched wreaths of red flowers draped the coffin. We buried a hero today—a man of God.

Rain fell unabated and washed over me—it seemed the heavens, too, were weeping. The rolling thunder above, like heralding trumpets, reminded me of a passage in *The Pilgrim's Progress* when Mr. Valiant-for-truth had been summoned by the King to the Celestial City. Before crossing the river, the valiant one said to those gathered about,

> "*My Sword* I give to him that shall succeed me in my Pilgrimage, and my *Courage* and *Skill* to him that can get it. My *marks* and *scars* I carry with me, to be a witness for me, that I have fought His battles, who now will be my Rewarder. When the day that he must go hence was come, many accompany'd him to the River-side, into which as he went, he said, *Death, where is thy Sting?* And as he went down deeper, he said, *Grave, where is thy Victory?* So he passed over, and all the Trumpets sounded for him on the other side."[3]

———

In more recent years, Pastor Stewart Custer was instrumental in the beginnings of Frontline Missions International. He and the other elders at my church encouraged me to set out on what would be the work of my life. In the start-up struggles, Dr. Custer was there and walked with me. Later, Danny Brooks was my pastor at Heritage Bible Church in Greer, South Carolina. When my family and I started attending Heritage, Danny was in the middle of preaching through the book of Matthew. I'll never forget his message on the crucifixion in chapter 27. I saw as never before the cost of grace and how I was not a spectator but had a part in what Jesus suffered. Newton's hymn came alive for me.

I saw one hanging on a tree
In agony and blood
Who fixed His loving eyes on me
As near His cross I stood
And never till my dying breath
Will I forget that look
It seemed to charge me with His death
Though not a word He spoke

My conscience felt and owned the guilt
And plunged me in despair
I saw my sins His blood had spilt
And helped to nail Him there
But with a second look he said
"I freely all forgive
this blood is for your ransom paid
I died that you might live"

Forever etched upon my mind
Is the look of Him who died
The Lamb I crucified
And now my life will sing the praise
Of pure atoning grace
That looked on me and gladly took my place.[4]

Danny's preaching powerfully and repeatedly made much of Jesus, and it caused us to want to make much of him, too. In fact, a number of people were sent out from the church to take the gospel to hard places where people lived and died without ever hearing the good news. As Danny often said from the pulpit, "The right question to ask isn't 'Why should I go?' but rather 'Why should I stay here?' That's the question we really need to wrestle with." Danny always preached to himself, and eventually he would also answer that question. In the middle of life, with two children in college and two in high school, it was a season that called for stability. But at the age of fifty, Danny left a thousand-member church that he had pastored for more than twenty years to take the gospel to the Salt Lake Valley in the middle of Mormon country. If Utah were on the Joshua Project's list,[5] it would rank among the gospel-destitute regions of the world. Others were already taking the gospel to this valley, but the few laborers matched with the scale of the abundance of the harvest cried out for more workers to come. So Danny Brooks walked the talk and went to Utah. I caught up with him and his wife, Kristen, a few months after they moved out to Utah to start a church.

Mormon Temple, Salt Lake City

### Salt Lake City, Utah
*December 1, 2017*

Drove into Salt Lake City this morning to Temple Square. Last night while driving this same route from the airport, I saw only the usual swirl of headlights, merging traffic, and malls huddled along the interstate. But this morning, the sun had cleared the tops of the snow-dusted Wasatch, flooding this vast valley with light. More than a million people live in the Salt Lake Valley. Danny pointed out one town after another that over the past twenty years have bulged out to form one seamless suburbia filling the valley.

Reached Temple Square late morning and took a guided tour of the complex. Danny and Kristen thought it would be good to have an introduction to Mormonism from Mormons. Danny said that when he brings guests here to visit, it's also a time for him to listen, learn, and pray for these blind guides.

Two Mormon missionaries, college-age women, led the tour. The first thing I noticed was their name tags. The name "JESUS CHRIST" was so big and bold you might have thought it was their name. Everything else was just fine print. This emphasis was the starting point of the tour as the two guides pointed out that Jesus Christ was at the heart of all they believe, as he is for all Christians. Portraits and mural paintings of Christ were everywhere. In a giant planetarium-looking room, a huge statue of Christ rose above us. It was very white, ghost-like.

Since their marketing pitch was that Mormons are Christians, I decided to test the waters and ask if I could ever go inside the Temple. The answer came quickly and almost in unison from the two guides: "No!" It turns out that only card-carrying Mormons can enter Mormon temples. This stop-you-at-the-door contradiction to the chameleon-like marketing of Mormonism is glaring. The Jesus that the Mormons here speak of isn't the Jesus of the Bible. The Jesus of the Bible is in the Bible. The Mormon Jesus is in *The Book of Mormon*. This Jesus was fabricated in the nineteenth century and is *a* son of God. He's the brother of Lucifer, and their father and mother came from another planet and started the process—a cosmic pyramid scheme whereby faithful Mormons can become gods themselves. And even have their own planet! I'm not making this up, but Joseph Smith sure did.

My heart hurts for these Mormon missionaries. I thought of the passage where Jesus said, "Many will say to me, 'Lord, Lord, did we not prophesy in your name . . . ?' And then will I declare to them, 'I never knew you'" (Matt. 7:22–23). Lord Jesus, give light to these guides who stumble about in the darkness of this place.

Afterwards, over lunch, I talked with Danny and Kristen about the spiritual challenges and gospel opportunities of this new world they've come to. I see so many parallels to Islam in Mormonism: not just in its patriarchal and polygamous aspects but also in how it diminishes the cross, dismisses the integrity of the Bible, and substitutes for Christ a new-and-improved prophet—whether Mohammed or Joseph Smith. Samuel Zwemer, the apostle to Islam, could just have easily been describing Mormonism when he wrote, "Islam is indeed the only anti-Christian religion. This world faith takes issue with everything that is vital in the Christian religion, because it takes issue in its attitude toward the Christ. By this it must stand or fall."[6] Danny is learning what he can about Mormonism, but he's not fixated on that. He's not here to win a "religion bee"—he's here to win souls through the power of the gospel. Danny said today, "You don't have to know everything about Mormonism to reach Mormons. What you have to know is the gospel." It's the same the world over. Mormonism, Islam, Buddhism, Hinduism, animism, atheism, or any other man-made religions are all just facades for lost people who are trying to save themselves.

## Temple Square, Salt Lake City
### December 2, 2017

Took a long walk downtown tonight to think. The air was cold and clear—so clear there were glimmers of the white-capped Wasatch in the distance. Temple Square was ablaze in Christmas lights, and big banners declared "A Savior Is Born!" A caroling troupe of Mormon missionaries from Brazil were singing Charles Wesley's "Hark! The Herald Angels Sing." The Temple itself glowed in soft white light, but to me it resembles a great sarcophagus. Behind the Temple is the Tabernacle, and the soothing sounds of the Mormon Tabernacle Choir spilled out and filled the crowded square with music. The promise of warmth and a pew where I could sit and write has drawn me inside the Tabernacle.

Nowhere is the chameleon-like character of Mormonism on display more than at Christmastime. After a richly orchestrated, pitch-perfect "O Holy Night," one of the Mormon "apostles" is now preaching. He started out by awarding Luke a brief honorable mention for providing us an account of the Christmas story, but after dispensing with this lip service, he went on to "another record" in *The Book of Mormon*. It was some of Joseph Smith's make-believe about Samuel the Lamanite and the Nephites in America at the time of Jesus's birth, etcetera, etcetera. The blind leading the blind, and the ditch here that they've fallen into is lined with Christmas lights, yet it is horribly dark.

Sitting here, seeing and hearing all this, has pulled back the curtain of memory for me to a time many years ago when I clearly and urgently shared the gospel with my Mormon aunt who was dying of cancer. It seemed as if I were describing the radiant wonder of a sunrise to a person born blind. Her funeral, which was presided over by her Mormon elders, was miserably hopeless, and the atmosphere as dismal as some of the Hindu temples I've been in. Standing there beside her casket with her dark priests mumbling their nonsense was the first time the reality of hell truly struck me. The death and blindness and darkness and lostness of the place stood in such stark contrast to the liberating, life-giving power of the cross-centered gospel.

This morning I gathered with some believers for a time of singing and sharing stories of gospel grace. We took joy in the worship of Jesus when we sang:

All the redeemed washed by His blood,
Come, and rejoice in His great love!
O praise Him! Alleluia!

Christ has defeated every sin.
Cast all your burdens now on Him!
O praise Him! O praise Him! Alleluia![7]

There are only about 2 percent evangelical Christians in a population of more than a million in the Salt Lake Valley, but the gospel works here, too. Men and women are shaking off the chains of Mormonism by the power and grace of God. I met a woman this morning who has experienced just such a deliverance. She shared with me her resignation letter from the Church of Jesus Christ of Latter-day Saints. The letter had such a Martin Lutheresque "here I stand" clarity about it! My newborn sister wrote to the Mormon bishop:

> I have given this matter considerable thought and prayer. I understand what you consider the "seriousness" and the "consequences" of my actions. I am aware that the church handbook says that my resignation "cancels the effects of baptism and confirmation, withdraws the priesthood held by a male member and revokes temple blessings." I also understand that I will be "readmitted to the church by baptism only after a thorough interview."
>
> I have come to this decision after careful study of the Bible, especially in the New Testament. I am convinced that the Bible is complete and that there was no apostasy, because Jesus Christ alone is the Head of the Church, and His words are completely trustworthy when He said that He would keep and preserve it. He said that "not even the gates of hell shall prevail against His church" (Matt. 16:18). I also believe that no man is good enough to have seen God, not even Joseph Smith (John 1:18). Since Jesus Christ is the only Mediator between God and man (1 Tim. 2:5), I can no longer look to self-appointed "Mediators" or "High Priests" in the LDS church. "Jesus Christ is the only Way, the Truth, and the Life, no man comes to the Father through anyone but Jesus Christ" (John 14:6). He is the Alpha and Omega, the Beginning and the End

(Rev. 1:8). The teachings of Mormonism are not the teachings of Christ, and I wish for you to read the New Testament in the Bible and find for yourselves the true teachings of the gospel. I believe in Jesus Christ alone for my salvation and that nothing I do can save me. This does not mean that I am not ready to work for God and do anything in my power to promote the gospel, but it means that those works are not what save me—only Jesus Christ has saved me from sin and death.[8]

May there be many more such liberation letters. May the mailboxes of Mormon churches, temples, and tabernacles be stuffed with them because of "all the Redeemed washed by His blood" who are now rejoicing in his great love! God, do this for your glory!

## Salt Lake Valley

### *December 3, 2017*

This morning Danny preached at a church in the south end of the valley to a gathering of about fifty. It was good to hear him open the Word again—it's been almost a year since I last heard him preach. He spoke of hopeful anticipation from 2 Peter 3. The promises that Peter refers to, drawing on Isaiah, give birth to our expectation of Jesus's coming and making all things right—peace, justice, and joy for his people forever! But Danny also pointed out the tension we have in that we are eager for Christ's return while asking for his patient mercy that more would come to faith.

Afterwards over coffee, I got to hear more about Danny and Kristen's journey to this place and how they could, as Martin Luther put it, "let goods and kindred go."[9] Danny said that the decision to leave their life and ministry in South Carolina to start over here was the accumulation of years of influences. One was hearing John Piper preach at T4G in 2008 on a passage in Hebrews 13:12–14, which struck Danny like an arrow. "So Jesus also suffered outside the gate in order to sanctify the people through his own blood. Therefore let us go to him outside the camp and bear the reproach he endured. For here we have no lasting city, but we seek the city that is to come." Then Piper said:

> My desire and prayer for you is that your life and ministry have a radical flavor. I say that for the glory of Christ. The world does not glorify Jesus as their supreme Treasure because of our health, wealth, and prosperity. Those are the same treasures they live for. The fact that we use Jesus to get what they want makes it clear to them that we have the same treasure as they do—and it is not Jesus. He's just the ticket. And tickets are thrown away when the show begins.
>
> What the world is waiting to see—what might awaken a sense of Christ's value—is something radical. Some risk. Some crazy sacrifice. Some extraordinary love. Something salty and bright. They may not like it when they see it. They may crucify it. But they will not be bored. Stephen's face shown like an angel (Acts 6:15). His wisdom was irresistible (Acts 6:10). So they killed him. But they did not yawn, and they did not go to sleep. And Acts 8 makes clear his death was not in vain. . . . When he bids us leave the securities and comforts of life and take up a radical, risk-taking, sacrificial way of love in his service, it is not a path that we take alone. In fact, Jesus is there outside the camp in a way that he is nowhere else. He is not just telling us to go out there. He is inviting us come out here. Here is where I am. Come to me outside the camp.[10]

That message was a definitive moment for Danny, but to what end? Was he just to stay put and fan the flames for others to go? He said after that he listened to Piper's message two or three times a year, but the tipping point came when an evangelist named Will Galkin, who was part of a church planting effort in Salt Lake City, told Danny, "This valley is dying for lack of the

Word," and asked him if he knew anyone who would be willing to come and plant a church. Danny said he didn't, but Will wasn't finished. "What about you? Will you pray about coming?"

Danny and Kristen

Danny couldn't refuse to at least pray, and so he and Kristen did—for months. They both said that was when the Scriptures came alive to them. As Danny put it, "The promises of God were like footers, as if God were pouring the concrete of his promises into our souls." Prayer, promises, and voices that seemed to call over and over—"This valley is dying for lack of the Word." "Let us go to him outside the camp." One Sunday morning at Heritage, Danny said he felt like Hudson Taylor did at Brighton Beach long ago. It was on a Sunday morning at church in Brighton when Taylor was so overcome at seeing "a thousand or more Christian people rejoicing in their own security, while millions were perishing for lack of knowledge"[11] that he walked out of church that morning to spend time in prayer and surrender. Danny didn't walk out of church, but it was becoming increasingly clear that he couldn't stay. Danny wasn't running away from something—he was running after Someone. "Let us go to him outside the camp."

Danny confessed that there had been a bit of idolatry in his life of leaning on and looking toward people and position. God loosened the soil around his roots, and repentance brought subsequent freedom to fully pursue what Jesus had ahead for him. Kristen, his amazing companion, was fully on board, and God gave her clear confirmations of her own. Once Danny came to a point of decision, she said "Well, then, let's go." So they did!

But the going was hard. Kristen said packing and moving was like a death. Her heart was raw and exposed. Moving day itself was especially hard as they loaded up their Subaru with two kids, a German Shepherd named Bristol, and stacks of stuffed Rubbermaid containers and set out for the two-thousand-mile drive west. Danny laughed that they looked like the Beverly Hillbillies. The most painful part was saying goodbye to their two older children, who remained in South Carolina, their parents, a lifetime of other family and friends, and a church family they had both given their lives to. Jesus said, "No one who puts his hand to the plow and looks back is fit for the kingdom of God" (Luke 9:62). That day, Danny put his hands on the steering wheel and, fighting tears, drove away. Along the way, God gave them reassuring reminders of his love through his people by giving them a warm coat, a meal, or a place for the night. But the sweetest gift of all was a note from Luke, their oldest son, that he posted while they were on the road:

> I don't have many words today. What really brings tears to my eyes more than the passage of life into the next phase, more than being the one to stay and not go, more than not being with my family anymore, are these words:
>
> "O wand'rer, come, on Him believe, His grace by faith receive. Awake, arise, and hear His call, the feast is spread for all."
>
> I cry because I have the privilege of experiencing the call and power of the gospel. I know that Christ will build his

church, and the powers of hell will not prevail against it. The feast is ready. The laborers are running to the ripened fields. We serve a great King.

I love you Dad, Mom, Hailey, and Seth. So proud of each of you.

As they recounted other stories of the move, I could see the stabs of joy and pain in their glistening eyes, but Danny said with a certain smile, "Jesus is worth it."

# 8

# Torn Curtain

## Roger Weil (London and Leningrad)

"One must be strong to place oneself alone against the unknown world."[1]

*Freya Stark*

Like a birthday best forgotten, the centennial of the Bolshevik Revolution in late 2017 passed with little notice. The events in Russia in 1917 set in motion the creation of the Soviet Union—the first state ever formally and violently committed to the complete re-creation of a society ordered by Marxism and atheism. The coup was but the first drops of a downpour, for what followed were "decades of murder on an industrial scale."[2] When the death toll at the hands of the Soviet regime, as well as in all the places where Communism spread (from China to North Korea, from Cambodia to Cuba), is counted, it is staggering: one hundred million.[3] That string of zeroes is the legacy of Soviet Communism and all the bloody wannabes that followed.

The devastations of World War II made many of the countries bordering the Soviet Union vulnerable to the Communist virus.

Winston Churchill said, as only Churchill could, "A shadow has fallen upon all the scenes so lately lighted by the Allied victory. . . . From Stettin in the Baltic to Trieste in the Adriatic, an iron curtain has descended across the Continent."[4] Churchill warned that the Communists were committed to "the indefinite expansion of their powers and doctrines."[5] And so it was. Eventually a third of the world's territory was under the hammer and sickle. The long Cold War that followed—East versus West, Communist versus free—was a struggle that dominated the world stage for more than a generation.

This bit of background is important to understanding the dangerous situation in which Christians behind the Iron Curtain were living and suffering. Pastors and Sunday school teachers were imprisoned—and some were executed. Church buildings were confiscated and turned into barracks, warehouses, and "museums of atheism." Bibles and other Christian literature were seized and destroyed.

Of course, all the efforts to stamp out the church then and now failed. From the first century to the twenty-first century, Gamaliel's cautionary counsel has mostly been ignored. In Acts 5 when Jewish rulers wanted to kill the disciples and silence the preaching of the resurrection of Jesus, Gamaliel warned his colleagues on the council, "I tell you, keep away from these men and let them alone, for if this plan or this undertaking is of man, it will fail; but if it is of God, you will not be able to overthrow them" (Acts 5:38–39). Empires from the Roman to the Soviet have come and gone, but the church of Jesus Christ remains because it is not the work of man but of God. I wish I could somehow communicate this reality to the Christ-hating dictators of our day, from the mullahs of the Middle East to the supreme leaders of China and North Korea. Stop trying to destroy the church. Your efforts are the classic definition of insanity: doing the same thing over and over again and expecting different results. The church belongs to Jesus. He purchased it with his own blood. All the Lenins, Stalins, and Maos put together are just dust.

As Christ continued to build his church in the Soviet Union and Eastern Europe, congregations grew. And with that, the pressing need for Bibles grew, too. The famine for the Bread of the Word was acute, and believers on both sides of the Iron Curtain responded. In 1967 the story of a Dutch evangelist known as Brother Andrew was published. *God's Smuggler* was a sensation and inspiration, as it described how Bibles were taken behind the Iron Curtain in Brother Andrew's Volkswagen. Of course, his remarkable story was just one of many such stories. Hundreds of men and women who never had a bestseller were also involved in smuggling Bibles and Christian literature. Most of them were not from the West but were Poles, Romanians, Lithuanians, Russians, and Ukrainians. They risked—and many lost—their freedom in order to print and smuggle Bibles to Christians. Printing presses were cobbled together from parts of washing machines and bicycles. Quantities of paper and ink had to be secured. Every step in making a book had to be done secretly—printing, collating, folding, stitching, trimming. And that was before the Bibles were even given to the couriers. These brave men and women sometimes carried heavy loads of books on trains or buses, traveling hundreds of miles day and night, all while they watched and prayed and played a high-risk cat-and-mouse game with the KGB.

A typewriter was an invaluable tool in many of these underground printing operations—but securing one was another matter. Couriers from the West often met this need. One of them was an unlikely smuggler, a young architect in the Queen's service in London, who would serve the persecuted church in the Soviet Union, Yugoslavia, and China for many years. But on one of his early forays behind the Iron Curtain, Roger Weil was confronted with real risk, paralyzing fear, and the power of the cross.

## London, England
### *October 20, 2014*

Late morning. Met up with Roger at Victoria Station. More than three years have passed since we were last together here at the old train station. My friend marked his eightieth birthday this summer, but he seemed just as energetic and joyful and engaged in the gospel cause as ever. Over cappuccinos, served in cups the size of soup bowls, we planned out our day—packing in as much walking, talking, history, and books as the day would permit. Being an architect by trade, he spent years working in the heart of London. Roger, therefore, knows every cornice and cobblestone in Westminster. I couldn't have a better guide, as he made the men who once walked these very streets come alive—from King Charles to Churchill. This really is one of my favorite cities in the world! The old wit, Samuel Johnson, said of the star-struck newcomers to this city that they believe they are "passing into another world, and images *London* as an elysian region, where every hour has its proper pleasure, where nothing is seen but the blaze of wealth, and nothing heard but merriment and flattery; where the morning always rises on a show, and the evening closes on a ball; where the eyes are used only to sparkle, and the feet only to dance."[6] Well, we didn't dance, but we did walk and talk, and our delightful day ran swiftly.

Roger was born in an affluent, close-knit, Jewish family. At eighteen, during his freshman year in architecture school, Roger was invited by a classmate to go to a Sunday evening service with him. Roger had never been to church before, so whether it was out of curiosity or courtesy, Roger accepted. The church was Westminster Chapel, and the pastor was Pastor Martyn Lloyd-Jones. His text that evening was Luke 9:56: "The Son of man is not come to destroy men's lives, but to save them" (KJV). Lloyd-Jones explained the difference between religion and Christianity and pointed out from the Scriptures God's patient warnings and provision of salvation. The preacher said that this is the central truth of the Bible and is why Jesus came—to save. Roger told me, "At once I understood that Christ's death on the cross was God's way of providing eternal forgiveness and peace. In my mind's eye, I saw him on the cross, and a wonderful peace entered my heart. Now I understood the truth of God's gospel!" As the Lord said in Isaiah, "Look unto me, and be ye saved, all the ends of the earth" (Isa. 45:22 KJV). The curtain of darkness was torn from top to bottom, and Roger looked and lived. And though over half a century has passed since that day, his eyes still glisten with tears of joy to tell of that night.

Roger Weil

As our day drew down and the sun drifted westward, we took a walk in St. James's Park. Moorhens shuffled about our path as we walked along a little lake, as swans glided over waters now golden. With Buckingham Palace crowning the western shore, I felt I was walking on a movie set of Masterpiece Theatre. Roger and I sat and talked, for I wanted to hear of the years when this mild-mannered architect was smuggling Bibles and typewriters into the U.S.S.R and other Communist countries. There's iron in the soul of this English gentleman. Hudson Taylor once wrote, "All God's giants have been weak men, who did great things for God because they reckoned on His being with them."[7] One of the stories was of the day Roger "reckoned" on God being with him. It was his day of days, long ago in Leningrad. I'll let Roger tell it in his own words:

In 1971, with the cold war between East and West still in deep freeze, I was making my second visit to the Soviet Union. Tourists were tightly controlled, and the cities we could visit were few in number. There was freedom of movement within the city limits—but under no circumstances outside them!

The previous year, by prior arrangement, I had met a pastor in Leningrad who had traveled from his hometown three hundred miles away to meet me. At that time he had asked me, if at all possible, to bring him on my next visit a new typewriter with a Russian language keyboard and Cyrillic characters. I promised to try. These were unobtainable to the ordinary Russian citizen, as the State strictly controlled all forms of communication, especially the printed page. At this time the Bible was a banned book, and Christian literature was prohibited. However, for those who were lucky enough to own a typewriter, things were different, even though there were no photocopiers! By inserting sheets of carbon between leaves of plain paper, a good typist could produce four or five copies of the original. In this way, albeit on a modest scale, *some* Christian literature could be made available!

So it was that in April 1971, I brought with me from England the specially made, brand-new typewriter! Its anonymous-looking carrying case had mercifully escaped notice coming through customs in Moscow. This time my visa allowed me to travel by plane from Leningrad to Tallinn, the city where the pastor lived. So far so good!

But an ominous dark shadow was soon cast over these proceedings. The day before my flight was due I discovered I was being followed everywhere I went. A stony-faced individual was undoubtedly dogging my steps! In an effort to get rid of him, I went down onto the crowded metro, but I could not shake him off. Evidently he was no amateur! To act as an innocent tourist, I decided to visit the world famous Hermitage Museum and Art Gallery, formerly the Czar's Winter Palace. Suddenly I remembered my typewriter sitting there in my hotel bedroom. What if the secret police who were following me were also investigating the luggage in my bedroom? What possible excuse had I for having a new Russian language typewriter? So who was it for and why did I bring it? To these questions I could give no satisfactory answers! A numbing fear crept over me, and my mouth went dry, and I could feel my heart pounding. How would I endure intense police interrogation, sleep deprivation, and possible physical suffering? Theoretically, I believed I would rather die than betray the pastor, but how would it be in reality? I could scarcely think straight or concentrate on the sumptuous surroundings and the magnificent paintings on the walls in front of me.

All at once I realized I was standing in front of a stark painting of the crucifixion. It stopped me in my tracks! I stared at it. More than that, "when I survey[ed] the wondrous cross on which the Prince of glory died,"[8] the cold cramping fear fell off my shoulders like a loose garment, replaced by the comforting warm glow of faith! I thought, "Fool to be afraid, you are in his hands, the one who died for you and rose again! All is well, safe in his care and keeping! Go on, go forward in faith therefore!"

Quietly and confidently I turned away, and without a backward glance, calmly walked back to my hotel to find my room undisturbed and in good order. All was well!

Next morning my typewriter and I took our flight to Tallinn to be met at the airport by the welcoming smile of the pastor! Mission accomplished, all praise to God!

As Roger and I walked back to Victoria Station to part ways, I rejoiced in the power of the cross and recalled Paul's words in Romans: "He who did not spare his own Son but gave him up for us all, how will he not also with him graciously give us all things?" I needed this word tonight. In the everlasting, ever-present, unshakeable refuge of the cross, I can (as Roger said) "Go on, go forward in faith!"

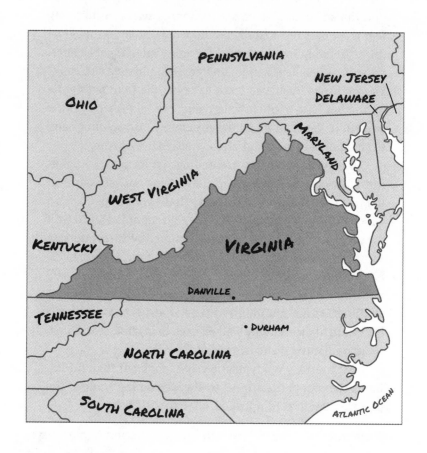

# 9

# White Rose

## Dollie Jones Keesee (Danville, Virginia)

"Everything we do in obedience to God, no matter how small,
is significant. It is part of a cosmic mosaic that God is painting
to display the greatness of his power and wisdom to the world
and to the principalities and powers in the heavenly places
(Ephesians 3:10). A deep satisfaction of the Christian life is that
we are not given over to trifles. Serving a widowed mother-in-
law, gleaning in a field, falling in love, having a baby—for the
Christian these things are all connected to eternity. They are
part of something so much bigger than they seem."[1]

*John Piper, speaking of Ruth*

Growing up, we had a Mother's Day tradition in my part of Virginia. At church on that Sunday, men and boys whose mothers
were still living would wear a red rose on their lapel, and any one
whose mom was deceased honored her by wearing a white rose.
That may explain why I have never liked white roses.

My earliest memories of my mother are bright ones. I remember how pretty she was, how much I liked her name, Dollie, and how much she and my dad loved each other. One thing she did not love, though, was travel. In that, she and I were very different. I don't believe she ever traveled more than two hundred miles from the place where she was born. Her interests were at home and not over some horizon. But as my world grew, she knew how to let me go. Like Hannah, she had dedicated her son to the Lord, which meant she had to let me go, even when it hurt. Mama took her part in the work and its risks by not holding onto me and by holding onto God. I remember she bought a globe and used it to trace the paths of my journeys and to pray. No matter where I went, whether in war zones or on long, lonely stretches of road or rail, her prayers for me were a constant force in my life.

Dollie Jones Keesee, Easter 1962: "Her hands were full."

Out of all the yellowing albums and shoeboxes of pictures, one of the photographs that best captures my mother's life is from an Easter Sunday long ago. As usual, her hands were full. In one hand, she is holding her Bible and a baby bottle. The Bible is cluttered with papers—and probably some sheet music—because she was both a Sunday school teacher and the church piano player. At our little church, she was a "Swiss Army knife" of servanthood. In the other hand, she (along with my older brother) holds the hand of my little sister, who was just learning to walk. I am the only one in the picture who isn't being useful.

Two more daughters were born in later years, and then grandchildren followed. Mama's hands were always busy: loving her husband, loving her children, comforting, correcting, cooking, cutting hair, reading, washing, and playing the old hymns—but with the style of Jerry Lee Lewis! On Saturday night, she used to practice for church the next day. She loved songs about heaven. She sang and banged them out in rapid rhythm, like she planned to be there. By God's grace, she made it. But to get there, he led her through years of suffering, as he stilled her busy hands. When she was dying of cancer, I wrote the following from her bedside.

## Durham, North Carolina
### *Early Morning, January 12, 2005*
The last bits of snow catch the light of a near full moon as it sets over cold, vacant streets. I was scheduled to be in Pakistan today, where I was to interview survivors of two church grenade bombings, but that trip was cancelled in order to be here—room 9331 of the cancer ward of Duke University Medical Center.

My mother, so thin now and so fragile, lies in a bed next to me. A tangle of tubes runs into her much-bruised arm. The machines she is attached to seem detached from her pain as they hum quietly to themselves. I sat through the night with her, catching a couple of naps during her shallow sleeping and shallow waking. She is resting now, and I am writing.

We had a good evening together yesterday, holding hands and reading much Scripture. My earliest memory of her was of her reading the Bible to my brother and me; so tonight it was my turn. With nearly forty years of teaching Sunday school, she taught many children besides her own about the Lord. Hers was always the quiet service in the back rooms—which is where much of the Lord's work is done. A pastor friend often repeated this saying, "Between the great things we cannot do and the little things we will not do lays the danger of doing nothing."[2] My mother, armed with flannelgraph, animal crackers, and Calvary love, was never in such danger.

We recalled tonight how we used to sing together. I was too young to read; so she taught me the words and played the piano. That old, beaten-up piano had a keyboard that looked like an ugly grin with ivories yellowed, cracked, or missing—but we sang the Lord's songs around it nonetheless. At church she played, too. I remember how pretty she was at the piano. She played, and I sang solos for special music of the songs she had helped me memorize. "Born to Serve the Lord" and "How Great Thou Art" were among the favorites, but she reminded me tonight that one of those songs that she taught me was about Stephen in Acts. I had forgotten that. Sitting here in this long hour before dawn, the words of the chorus all come back:

> I see Jesus standing at the Father's right hand.
> I see Jesus yonder in the Promised Land.
> Work is over, now I am coming to Thee.
> I see Jesus standing, waiting for me.[3]

She cannot sing now behind the oxygen mask with her throat parched by radiation, but she did tell me in the middle of the night that there are times lately when she has heard the most beautiful music.

The east brightens. Mama is stirring. She asks to be propped up so she can see the morning sky.

## Iloilo, Central Philippines

### *May 14, 2006*

A typhoon delayed our flight yesterday from Manila to Iloilo by several hours, but despite the winds and driving rain, our Cebu Pacific flight took off into the dark sky. We prayed and committed our way to the Lord, who can speak, "Peace, be still!" to the storm. Other than hitting a few "washboards" on the way and getting kicked sideways once, we bounced into the Iloilo airport last evening in good shape.

This morning the sky is clearing. Beyond the coconut palms, the blue mountains of Iloilo rise above the swirling mist. It is my birthday—and it is Mother's Day. It has been a year since Mama was taken from our arms into the arms of the Lord. The grief and separation are still fresh. She would not be surprised to find me here on a little island far away in the South Pacific, though. We were always close, though often I was far away. I guess it is still that way . . .

On Mama's last birthday, I gave her a dozen red roses. She died the next day, and I slipped one of them into her hand. At her funeral, my brother, sisters and I scattered the last red petals on her casket—fragrant bits of life cast into the grave, a promise of things to come. I know through the power of the risen Christ that Mama has never been more alive and her hands never more busy as she serves and praises in the place she so often sang about and now sees—a place where all tears have been wiped away by nailed-scarred hands and where no one ever wears the white rose of sorrow.

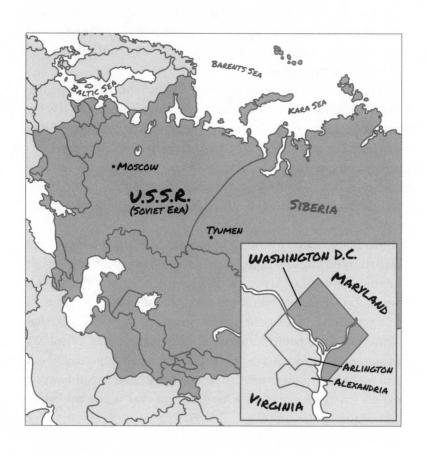

# 10

# Cell 44

## Georgi Vins (Soviet Union)

"I am not alone here. My brothers in the faith are in many neighboring cells. Even within these walls God is strengthening our faith and inspiring radiant hope in our hearts! Christ is unconquerable."[1]

*Georgi Vins*

First light had just begun to finger its way through the thick cold forests of Tyumen. Though it was already late April, this lonely stretch of Siberia seemed to take little notice of the calendar. Ice still clung to the rivers, and dirty snow remained piled up about the prison grounds. Inside the crowded gulag, prisoners huddled on the concrete floor, clinging to their last moments of sleep— or more like a restless rest—because of the thick air, the latrine stench, the bloody coughs, and the skin-crawling sense of lice.

Beneath one of the blankets was Georgi Vins, a Baptist preacher who had already spent eight years in prison for preaching the gospel. When the ice cleared the river, he would finish his sentence but would have yet five more years of exile in the Arctic wilds of northern Siberia. At least his family could join him there, but his health was broken. Could he survive? He had seen his youngest child only once in five years. How would they live? And what of his dear Christian friends, his fellow pastors, the secret Bible printing teams? So many troubled thoughts and dark fears swirled about him.

The eastern sun brightened the grimy, barred windows of the cell. The heavy lock clanked. The door opened, and a guard shouted out to the stirring shapes on the floor, "Vins, get your things and come with me!"

Soviet prison camp

Let's hit pause at this moment. It's April 1979 in a Soviet gulag in Tyumen in central Siberia—just one prison among the hundreds scattered across the Soviet Union's eleven time zones—what Aleksandr Solzhenitsyn famously called the *gulag archipelago*. These prisons held the usual assortment of thieves, rapists, and murderers, along with others who had committed crimes against the state, like Sunday school teachers and pastors. Among them was Russian Baptist pastor Georgi Vins (1928–1998), a key leader among the evangelical Baptist churches in the Soviet Union. Vins organized secret Bible printing teams and traveled widely to encourage the underground church. He was first arrested in Moscow in 1966 for delivering a petition to the government asking for the release of hundreds of Christian prisoners. He served a three-year sentence but was arrested again in 1974. This time he was sentenced to five years in prison to be followed by another five years in exile.

John Piper said, "God is always doing 10,000 things in your life, and you may be aware of three of them."[2] At this particular moment on the morning of April 26, 1979, Georgi Vins could perhaps see less than three as he made his way out of his prison cell. However, God was doing ten thousand things at once across the world on behalf of his servant so that this imprisoned pastor—and Christians on both sides of the Iron Curtain—could say with the psalmist, "When the LORD restored the fortunes of Zion, we were like those who dream. Then our mouth was filled with laughter, and our tongue with shouts of joy; then they said among the nations, 'The LORD has done great things for them'" (Ps. 126:1–2).

The following entries, drawn from the diaries and memoirs of a prisoner and a president, record the unfolding events and remind us of the power of our God "who is able to do immeasurably more than all we ask or imagine" (Eph. 3:20 NIV).

### Georgi Vins, Tyumen, U.S.S.R.
*April 26, 1979*

"The next day, guards inform me that I was being moved to Moscow. I was alarmed. What had happened? My place of exile was near Tyumen. The reply was customary: 'You're a prisoner and not allowed to ask questions. Just get ready.' . . . *This is certainly strange*, I thought, *What's going on? Am I going to be tried again? Maybe some other Christian leaders were arrested and there will be a joint trial and I'll be sentenced again.* That was the only logical explanation I could think of for my transfer to Moscow. I couldn't sleep that night. I prayed a lot and again committed my life into the Lord's hands."[3]

## President Jimmy Carter, White House
### April 26, 1979

"We have completed the negotiations with the Soviets on the prisoner exchange. I think we've got an excellent deal, having Ginzburg and Vins, plus three others, released from the Soviet Union. . . . They've also agreed not to execute . . . one of our spies who had been condemned to die. In return for this, we commuted the sentences of two United Nations minor spies [Soviets] who were convicted last year."[4]

## Georgi Vins, Moscow, U.S.S.R
### April 27, 1979

"A guard woke me early and told me to shower. The first thing in the morning? I was really surprised. Nothing like this ever happened before in my prison life. . . .

"After a while, the captain returned. 'Follow me!' he ordered, and led me down the corridor to an office. As I went in he disappeared down the hall. Behind a desk sat a high-ranking official. He stood and handed me a document.

"'Read this,' he said.

"It was a decree from the Presidium of the Supreme Soviet of the U.S.S.R. stating that I was being stripped of my Soviet citizenship and would be exiled to the United States of America.

"Silence filled the room. The official looked at me. 'Do you understand that you're being expelled from the territory of the Soviet Union and that you are no longer a citizen of the U.S.S.R.?' he asked.

"'I understand,' I said, 'but I don't agree to this. Can a person really be deprived of his citizenship and exiled from his homeland because of religious activities?'

"The official cut me off, saying that the decision had been made by the highest authority in the country and the matter was now closed. Then he informed me that in two hours I would no longer be on Soviet soil.

"'You are the most unfortunate person in the world,' he added condescendingly. 'You are a man with no citizenship, no homeland, no roots. You're being sent to America. Maybe for a week or two you'll cause quite a sensation there, but soon everyone will forget about you. Nobody there needs you.'

"The guards whisked me and four other prisoners onto an Aeroflot jet. A Soviet medical doctor was assigned to travel with us, and twenty plainclothes KGB agents guarded us on that flight to New York. After we were seated, civilian passengers boarded the plane.

"We prisoners were not allowed to speak to anyone during the ten-hour flight. So many thoughts crowded my weary mind as I stared out the window. *Lord, why are You taking me to this foreign country? I don't know anyone in America. I don't speak English. What will it be like? When will I see my family again?*"[5]

### President Jimmy Carter, White House
#### April 28, 1979

"The five prisoners were awakened at 4:00 in the morning in their individual prison cells. All given practically no notice, but informed that their Soviet citizenship was revoked—that they would have to leave the Soviet Union. They were given minimal details about the substance of the exchange, informed that their families would not be punished and might be joining them, and then were transferred to an Aeroflot plane."[6]

### Georgi Vins, New York
#### April 28, 1979

"After the plane landed at Kennedy Airport in New York, we five prisoners and our guards remained seated while the other

147

passengers got off the plane. Then the plane taxied to an isolated runway and we were ordered to leave the aircraft. The guards didn't follow us. Although we didn't know it at the time, at the same moment two Soviet spies captured by the Americans were boarding through a different door. Later we learned that an agreement had been negotiated between President Jimmy Carter and Premier Leonid Brezhnev to exchange five prisoners for the two spies.

"Several officials from the U.S. State Department met us as soon as our feet touched American soil and congratulated us on our freedom. Then we were taken by car to a Hilton Hotel. Each of us was given a private room on the 36th floor. When I found a Bible on my nightstand, I thought that probably the Americans had put one in my room because they knew I was a Christian. Unfortunately, it was in English. I mentioned this to a State Department official and later that night an anonymous New Yorker brought me a Russian Bible. After five years, I finally had my own Bible!

Georgi Vins's first morning in America
with his treasured Russian Bible

"The next morning, newspaper, radio, and television correspondents arrived to interview us. Later that day at a large press conference, each of us former prisoners made a statement through an interpreter. When my turn came, I lifted my Russian Bible high and said, 'I'm the happiest person in the world. I now have my own Bible and no one will take it away from me!'

"I could tell by their expressions that the journalists didn't understand what was so special about having a Bible. They didn't know what it meant for a Christian to go many years without God's Word.

"President Carter saw that news program and wanted to meet me, so later that day I flew to Washington, D.C., accompanied by representatives of the State Department and an interpreter."[7]

## President Jimmy Carter, White House
### April 28–29, 1979

"The prisoner exchange was very successful and a highly emotional experience for all those who were there . . . it's one of the most significant things in a human way that we've done since I've been in office.

"We treated the dissidents with great respect, gave them optimum opportunity for freedom (which they did not take), took them to a fairly luxurious hotel. We then let some Ukrainian leaders come in to see Moroz, and some Jewish leaders come in to see the three Jewish dissidents. Vins was quite remorseful that he had left the Soviet Union, even though his family is going to follow him. He felt that the Baptists and other Christians there should not have been abandoned by him. . . .

"I was to teach Sunday School the next morning, and our pastor, Reverend Charles Trentham, invited Vins to worship with us. . . . I told Vins not to feel guilty about being sent from the Soviet Union, because he had already had an opportunity to send a Christian message to the ten million television viewers who saw him raise his Bible when he arrived in the United States. He was still concerned about his family, and I informed him that President Brezhnev had promised me that there would be no delay or obstacles in having the families reunited."[8]

## Georgi Vins, Washington, D.C.
### *April 29, 1979*

"On Sunday morning, I met President Carter at the First Baptist Church. We had a twenty-minute conversation, during which I presented the situation of the persecuted believers in my homeland and told him about those who remained in prisons, labor camps, and psychiatric hospitals for their faith.

Walking to church with President Carter
Courtesy of the Jimmy Carter Library

"President Carter invited me to his Sunday school class. I sat between Mrs. Carter and an interpreter. About one hundred people listened as the President opened God's Word and taught a lesson from the book of Esther. He also spoke about my release. 'We've prayed for many years for Georgi Vins, our brother in Christ,' he said. 'God has answered our prayers. It was neither I nor the Congress nor the American negotiators who freed him. God himself did it and He deserves all the credit.'

"I marveled at the United States president holding a Bible in his hands, treating it with respect and teaching from it. How different from the leaders in my own country who were confiscating and burning Bibles and putting Christians in prison for preaching from that book! I will never forget that day."[9]

### President Jimmy Carter, White House
*April 30, 1979*
"These five were really an impressive group in their diversity and also in their commitment. I think the Soviets underestimated the impact of their release on American and world opinion."[10]

---

When Georgi Vins was released from prison and came to America, the fall of the Berlin Wall and the dissolution of the Soviet Union were in the future. Yet like a stone that starts an avalanche, Georgi Vins's freedom was a foretaste of the freedom that millions would experience when the Communist regimes were shaken to their very foundations a decade later.

Crisscrossing the globe, Georgi Vins went right to work on behalf of the persecuted church. Challenging Christians on four continents, he gave voice to the suffering believers behind the Iron Curtain. Even after freedom came, Vins continued to strengthen churches in Russia and Ukraine by training pastors, building churches, and evangelizing widely.

The release of Georgi Vins from a Soviet prison was a sovereign surprise, God himself answering the question, "Is there anything too hard for the Lord?" It was also a reminder of the profound power of prayer. One evidence of that truth is captured in an unexpected letter I received several years ago:

Dear Friends,

I can never look at Georgi Vins' name without thinking of my second son, Joel. When my wife and I had only two boys (we have been blessed with four), we adopted a practice of choosing one missionary each, four in total, to pray for from a bulletin board in the kitchen that we had filled with prayer cards. For some reason Joel often prayed for Georgi Vins. At that time he was in prison, and you are well aware of his circumstances. I personally thought his situation was hopeless and that he would die a martyr's death in prison. It pained me to hear Joel pray night after night for something so hopeless. I wanted, as people of little faith do, to pray for things that God would really consider doing. I was afraid that Joel would learn that God didn't really answer prayer.

I will never forget hearing of Georgi Vins' release. The thought still brings me to tears. God answers prayer. He answers it according to His marvelous purposes wrought before the foundation of the world. But—somehow—the prayers of the saints play a part, even the prayers of a little boy touched by the sight of a gaunt, haggard spiritual giant of a man called to preach the gospel in the very stronghold of evil.[11]

Many like young Joel tugged on the hem of God's garment, and the Lord answered their faith by moving mountains. Georgi Vins's story reminds us of who our God is!

I met Georgi Vins in 1996, just before my first trip to Russia and Ukraine. Unbeknownst to either of us, this would be the beginning of my ministry with the churches in the former Soviet Union that he loved and served so well for so long. Also unbeknownst to us was that our first meeting would be our last. A little more than a year later, Georgi Vins died after a brief struggle with cancer. The exile was finally home. The man without a country had indeed found "a better country" (Heb. 11:16).

No doubt waiting to greet him were fellow prisoners, former criminals who were ransomed by the Friend of sinners, for Vins often spoke the gospel with urgency and compassion to the worst of men in the worst of places—and many believed! The apostle Paul wrote from a prison cell, "I want you to know, brothers, that what has happened to me has really served to advance the gospel" (Phil. 1:12). Georgi Vins lived that verse. He knew its truth in every sense. He could hear it, smell it, and see the crowded faces of prisoners and guards. One of those places was known as Cell 44. There in the midst of his own suffering, he found sudden joy in seeing God open prison doors and prisoners' hearts to the gospel. Here's his story—his own prison epistle from Cell 44:

> When I was arrested for religious activity and denied the work for which I consecrated my life, I lost heart. I was put in a cell with approximately one hundred other people after my first interrogation. Suddenly I understood why I was in prison. Before going to bed I prayed, "Lord, it used to be so difficult for me to gather people together in order to preach your gospel. But now I have no need to gather them. They are already here. Make me a blessing to them. . . ."
>
> The Lord heard my prayer. Prisoners were coming and going through this cell. In a short time forty people believed in Christ. I taught them to sing hymns and pray. Guards often banged on the door and ordered us to be silent. The authorities finally found out what was happening and transferred me to the cell for hardened criminals. Precisely at that time, I received from my family a parcel containing bread, sugar, and clothing. When I entered the new cell, the criminals' eyes searched me. I took a few steps, set my bag on the floor, and looked around at them.
>
> "Men, today I received a parcel. Maybe there are some needy among you. Divide it."
>
> A tall, sullen fellow, probably their leader, approached me, silently took my parcel, and divided it equally among all of us. "Here, this is your part," he said, giving me a portion and returning my empty bag.

As a newcomer, I had to take the worst place in the cell, but the leader said, "For good people we have a good place. Now tell us why they transferred you to this cell."

"Well, in cell 44 I taught people how to pray to God. The authorities did not like it, so they threw me in here."

The leader smiled for the first time. "Very good! Now you will teach us."[12]

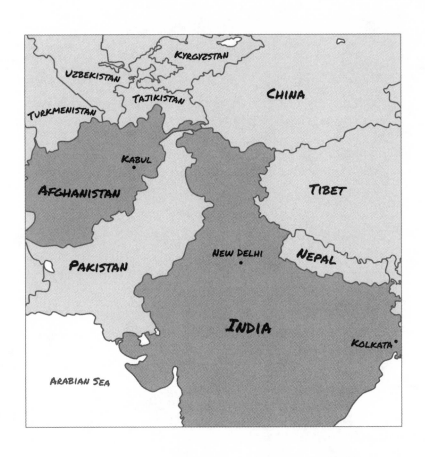

# 11

# Martyrdom of Faithful

## Gayle and Cheryl (Afghanistan)

"You speak in your letter of the possibility of one place being safer than another; I think, dear Eva, from the human standpoint all are equally unsafe, from the point of view of those whose lives are hid with Christ in God all are equally safe! . . . 'A mighty fortress is our God,' and in Him we are safe for time and for eternity. Shall we murmur if we have less of time than we expected?"[1]

*Edith Searell, missionary to China, in one of her last letters before dying in the Boxer Rebellion*

When John Bunyan describes martyrdom in his allegory *The Pilgrim's Progress*, he helps us look beyond "the things that are seen" to "the things that are unseen" (2 Cor. 4:18). In one of the most vivid scenes in the book, Christian and Faithful are nearing the City of Vanity. As the two pilgrims approach the town, they receive encouragement and direction from a guide named

Evangelist. He leaves them with these words of counsel: "Believe steadfastly concerning things that are invisible."[2] This insight soon becomes clear as the pilgrims enter the city. They arrive on market day to a lively scene of shops and street stalls well-stocked with every customer's every desire. But the carnival-like atmosphere of Vanity Fair quickly turns dark and hostile when Christian and Faithful refuse to buy anything; and the foreignness of their dress, speech, and allegiance sets them apart for mockery and assault. The unwelcome travelers are arrested, and a sham court is quickly assembled. Faithful's testimony of devotion to his King and his defiance of the prince of that city brings down upon him the full rage of his captors. What follows is a mob scene of unrestrained hate as they fall upon Faithful in an instant, beating him with their fists, piercing him with swords, crushing him with stones, and then burning his body to ash.

By all appearances, injustice had won. The enemies of the King had forever silenced the voice of one of his witnesses—at least, it seemed that way. But here Bunyan pulls back the curtain "concerning things that are invisible." He points past the blood-spattered scene, swirling with fire and ash and faces concentrated on killing, to something beyond: "Now I saw, that there stood behind the multitude a Chariot and a couple of horses waiting for Faithful, who (so soon as his adversaries had dispatched him) was taken up into it and straightway was carried up into the clouds with the Sound of Trumpet, the nearest way to the Celestial Gate."[3]

There are two realities in view. In the foreground is violent martyrdom, but beyond that scene the horses of heaven are waiting to bring the faithful witness to a swift, glorious welcome home.

> Sing, Faithful, Sing, and let thy Name survive;
> For tho' they kill'd thee, thou art yet alive.[4]

The death and deliverance of Faithful at Vanity Fair is a composite picture that Bunyan draws from a great company of martyrs—witnesses who were sure that neither death nor life would be able to separate them from the love of God in Christ Jesus their Lord. Like them, we too can take risks, face fear, and endure suffering with death-defying joy because Jesus is alive and with his people *always*. This is how Mary Slessor, a pioneer missionary to the interior of Africa, put it:

> I do not like that petition in the Prayer Book, From sudden death, good Lord, deliver us. I never could pray it. It is surely far better to see Him at once without pain of parting or physical debility. Why should we not be like the apostle in his confident outburst of praise and assurance, "For I am persuaded . . ."? Don't talk about the cold hand of death—it is the hand of Christ.[5]

The Christian's way of life is rooted in the reality of the resurrection. Gospel messengers who brave hostile places don't go to seek martyrdom. Rather they go to fully live for the glory of Christ and the sake of others, and they trust that the timing and circumstances of their departure are in God's hands. And they are in good hands! As the Puritan Thomas Watson put it, "We are more sure to arise out of our graves than out of our beds."[6]

The Christian's culture of life is in stark contrast to the culture of death that animates militant Islam. This violent strain of Islam celebrates religion-based killing as a rite and includes suicide-bombers in their arsenal.[7] Into this culture of death, Christians go, armed only with Calvary love and a life-giving message. They carry out the radical rescue work of the gospel through acts of mercy and words of witness. I saw this in Afghanistan in the lives—and deaths—of Gayle Williams and Cheryl Beckett. Gayle was a physical therapist who lived and worked in Afghanistan, helping to rehabilitate children maimed by landmines. She had served in a clinic in Kandahar for two years until her team was forced to leave because of the deteriorating security situation. She then relocated to Kabul to continue serving disabled children. Cheryl Beckett worked in Afghanistan for six years as a community development worker and Pashto interpreter. She spent her time there reaching, loving, and serving Afghan women. In that deeply segregated society characterized by the Pashtun saying "A woman's place is in the home or in the grave,"[8] Cheryl could cross that barrier and befriend the women behind the burqas. She helped Afghan women plant gardens and fruit trees, and along the way she planted gospel seeds, too. When I first visited Kabul, Cheryl was already a veteran worker of four years who led by example through her quiet courage, contagious joy, and intimate prayer life. Beth, who served there with my organization, was one of those whom Cheryl mentored. Even after Cheryl's death, the fragrance of Christ lingers on in the lives of teammates such as Beth. Because Jesus is alive and our lives are forever bound up in his life, death is no longer the worst thing that can happen. As Tim Keller said, "Resurrection is not just consolation— it is restoration. We get it all back—the love, the loved ones, the good, the beauties of this life—but in new, unimaginable degrees of glory and joy and strength."[9] And so, like Faithful at Vanity Fair, in the face of untimely graves and unanswered questions, Gayle, Cheryl, and a great host of whom the world is not worthy, continue to teach us to "believe steadfastly concerning things that are invisible."

## Kabul, Afghanistan
*October 20, 2008*

As the sun sinks over Kabul, a *muezzin* chants out the *azan* from a nearby mosque. Its cant sounds especially piercing and sinister to me, like the cackle of a demon. Blood calls out from the ground, for this morning Gayle Williams was gunned down by the Taliban just a few streets away. She was shot as she walked to work.

Kabul, Afghanistan

As soon as Beth and I heard the news, we went over to the elementary school to watch the children of the Christian workers while they worked on implementing a lockdown, since it is evident that foreign aid workers are being targeted for assassination. The last time we were together a few days ago, we were all worshiping along with Gayle. Today we were sorrowing together.

The Taliban claimed credit for the killing, declaring Gayle guilty of the crime of "spreading Christianity." And so she joins the ranks of Stephen and countless others—those "of whom the world was not worthy" (Heb. 11:38). Now Gayle stands in light, her wounds healed by wounded hands, safe, comforted, and home. That's how it looks on the other side of the thin line of life. On this side, though, there are questions, sorrow, and blood on a back street in Kabul.

> Why, O LORD, do you stand far away?
>> Why do you hide yourself in times of trouble? . . .
> For the wicked boasts of the desires of his soul, . . .

161

He sits in ambush in the villages;
>in hiding places he murders the innocent. . . .
Arise, O LORD; O God, lift up your hand;
>forget not the afflicted.
Why does the wicked renounce God
>and say in his heart, 'You will not call to account'?
But you do see . . .
>that you may take it into your hands;
to you the helpless commits himself. . . .
Break the arm of the wicked and evildoer;
>call his wickedness to account. (Psalm 10)

### October 24, 2008

Gathered with workers for a worship service held at a nearby house this morning. Despite Gayle's murder this week and all the subsequent threats, the main prayer request was, "Pray that our agencies back home won't make us leave."

The gathering was a tender time, too, as we remembered Gayle's life—Christlike to the end. It seems the Lord was preparing her for home, because after the kidnapping of a coworker two months ago, she told a friend that, though shaken, she was prepared to die in Afghanistan. Tomorrow she will be buried here, and another cross will be raised in this place—a kingdom stake driven into this barren land by the indisputable power of Calvary love. Even the gates of hell creak and shudder and will be crushed by the force of it.

Nate, a team leader and coworker with Gayle, closed our worship time by playing a song from his iPod. I had never heard it before; now I can never forget it. The words, like an unspoken prayer, gave voice to all that was within my heart.

I surrender all to You
The past the years to come right now
With every breath I bring to You
My hopes and fears and long discarded dreams.

Take them from my trembling hands
Before I lose my nerve and change my mind
Tear to shreds my safety net
And rip up every back up plan I make.

Though I do not see You now
I will turn my back on every doubt
And I am going to trust that You
In Your own time will work it out.

Empty hands bring peace of mind
Your burden is far lighter than my own
And every step I take to You
Leads me ever closer still to home.[10]

## Kabul Airport
### *November 6, 2008*

I woke at 4:30 this morning. No lights. The generator is down. I took a lantern to keep from stumbling with my pack. The light danced along the stone walls beneath the fading stars as the *azan* echoed in the quiet, cold streets of Kabul. I got a quick breakfast, tossed down some coffee, and set out for the airport.

There was a gauntlet of checkpoints to navigate, and then a maze of razor wire. Search points ringed the passage into the airport perimeter. I've lost track of how many times I've been patted down and my pack rifled through just to get to this gate. Now I wait for my flight to Delhi—and then home—so it's a good time to catch up on my journal.

Yesterday I said my goodbyes to Cheryl and Beth and our Dutch friends Annetta and Joop at a coffee shop where the cappuccinos were good and the customer service even better. Guards with guns at the ready scouted the perimeters and escorted us to and from our vehicles. Along the way to coffee, we passed the wreckage from a suicide bombing a few days ago. Tarps covered the spattered street, and the face of a building was simply torn away.

Before parting ways, I asked Joop if he would take us to the British Cemetery, also called the Christian Cemetery. It's a high-walled half-acre where soldiers, wanderers, and not a few missionaries are buried. Gayle's grave is the newest here—a mound of dust marked with wreaths of fading flowers and a cross fashioned out of pink ribbon. It seemed so desolate. We sat on nearby tombstones and took it all in. Cheryl was a good friend of Gayle's and said little. There wasn't much to say. Though our voices choked with sorrow, the stones seemed to cry out and declare Christ's glory. I noticed on one of the old tombstones near Gayle's grave there were carved in bold letters in English and in Dari, "He is not here. He is risen." The angel's words to the weeping were a needed reminder of another reality far removed from this war and this untimely grave—endless life, endless joy because "he is not here. He is risen."

British Cemetery, Kabul

## Kabul, Afghanistan
### *June 11, 2010*

Awoke at 3:30 this morning to the annoying call to prayer crackling over a loudspeaker from a nearby mosque. I'm sure those things must be a recording on a timer, for who in their right mind would be up and waking everyone else up so early?

Actually, it gave me a needed and precious two hours before daybreak of prayer and rejoicing in Jesus—his cross, his love. The lines of one song I listened to were particularly perfect for the moment.

> On such love, my soul, still ponder,
> Love so great, so rich, so free;
> Say, while lost in holy wonder
> "Why, O Lord, such love to me?"
> Hallelujah! Grace shall reign![11]

It was a needed reminder, for these have been difficult days of threats, searches, imprisonments, and narrow escapes for believers here. Yesterday I had lunch with Beth at Cheryl's house, and we ate BLTs. Where Cheryl got contraband bacon in this city is anyone's guess! We had a good time together, and laughter lightened our hearts. However, the pressure and weariness of these heavy days showed on Cheryl's face.

Last night we gathered for prayer in a house just around the corner from the spot where Gayle was murdered by the Taliban over a year ago. Her blood still stains the wall where they shot her. After the meeting, they were sorting books to burn so they don't fall into the hands of the police. As the noose of house searches and interrogations tightens, there have been more and more books and papers to burn. I think the birthday present Beth gave me yesterday was one that she spared from the fire. I'm glad for it because neither of us could have stood to see a dear old Samuel Zwemer book go up in flames. Yet Dr. Zwemer would have understood, for he himself wrote over a century ago:

> When you read in reports of troubles and opposition, of burning up books, imprisoning colporteurs, and expelling workers, you must not think that the Gospel is being defeated. It is conquering. What we see under such circumstances is only the dust in the wake of the ploughman. God is turning the

world upside down that it may be right side up when Jesus comes. He that plougheth should plough in hope. We may not be able to see a harvest yet in this country, but furrow after furrow, the soil is getting ready for the seed.[12]

That kingdom vision in Revelation of the ransomed from every tribe and language and nation gathered in joyful worship is a staggering vision. But here today in the wake of the ploughman, it's a vision dimmed by dust, smoke, and blood-stained walls.

## Somewhere over the Atlantic Bound for India
*September 3, 2010*

Another night flight before me. I feel a bit like the crumpled plane tickets by which I measure my days. It's been a season of journeys and a season of sorrow. With the killing of friends in Afghanistan in recent days, it has raised questions that no Christian cliché can answer. I think of the lines of an old hymn,

> The thorns in my path are not sharper
> than composed His crown for me.
> The cup that I drink not more bitter
> Than He drank in Gethsemane.[13]

And so I will follow him to be like him.

I had scheduled months ago to be in India to travel with my pastor friend Aashish to Kolkata and visit several gospel outposts in the north of the country. But it's also good that I am here now in the wake of our sorrows in Afghanistan so that I can see my friend Beth, who is hurting.

## Delhi, India
*September 11, 2010*

A downpour in Delhi matches my mood. Met up with Beth last night. I had asked her to make arrangements to come out of Kabul to meet me here and talk through her sorrow. Several of her coworkers were killed recently when ten Christian aid workers were ambushed and murdered by Islamic militants. They were providing medical services out in Nuristan, one of the hardest and most neglected regions of Afghanistan. Our friend and Beth's mentor Cheryl was among them. She was a beautiful soul who never failed to lift my spirits with her joy in Christ. Our time together in June was precious, although at the time I didn't realize just how precious. I don't expect a good answer to why at thirty-two years of age she should be taken. She brought so much strength to the team, and she poured the love of Jesus into the Afghan people. There are already so few there—so few willing to go there.

Cheryl Beckett

It's hard for me to write about her. I'm going to miss her and miss hearing her pray. Cheryl had a way of praying as if she were talking to her best friend. Now she is with him; she never took her eyes off him. A few days ago, Beth shared a song that Cheryl wrote, which is drawn from Isaiah 43:

The waters came today, the rivers ran deep.
I saw the waves today; I watched them crashin' over me.
I was drownin' in despair, and I couldn't get up for air.
Then I heard Your voice callin' out to me:

Fear not! I have redeemed you.
Fear not! For I have summoned you by name.
I'm takin' you by the hand, I've placed your feet upon dry
    land,
I will be with you, You will not be swept away.

I felt the burn today, saw the flames beneath my feet,
Walkin' through the fire today, I can't take this heat.
I am drownin' in despair and can't get up for air—
Then I hear Your voice callin' out to me:

Fear not! I have redeemed you.
Fear not! For I have summoned you by name.
You are precious in my sight, so don't give up this fight.[14]

She "being dead yet speaketh" (Heb.11:4 KJV)—"don't give up this fight." Lord, look now on your servant Beth and give healing to her heart and strength as she feels the weight of the cross she now embraces.

## Rajdhani Express, Delhi to Rajasthan
*September 13, 2010*

Another night train—my friend Aashish and I are westward bound. Before leaving Delhi, we parted with Beth. We both know the dark cloud that she is flying back into as she returns to a war zone and empty places at the table. She gave me a letter this morning, including a portion of Psalm 27:

> Tim,
> Last year in October when I left for Afghanistan, you gave
> me the verses in Isaiah 43 (1–13) with the promises that I would

not be overwhelmed by the waters and I would not be burned by the fire. His promises have held true, even though there is pain. I am grateful you were able to take the time to give me what I needed most right now: presence. I am grateful that you like the Timothy of the Bible came to establish and exhort me in my faith, that I wouldn't be moved by these afflictions (1 Thess. 3:2–3). I've written here my verses of promise from Psalm 27 because I wanted to remind you (and me) that I *can* go back into the midst of the army that is "encamped around me" because He has promised that He *will* shelter me in my day of trouble. If I didn't have this promise, I wouldn't go. But I do, so I can go with confidence. May He hem you in.

—Beth

Psalm 27

The Lord is my light and my salvation;
    whom shall I fear?
The Lord is the stronghold of my life;
    of whom shall I be afraid?
When evildoers assail me
    to eat up my flesh,
my adversaries and foes,
    it is they who stumble and fall.
Though an army encamp against me,
    my heart shall not fear;
though war arise against me,
    yet I will be confident.
One thing have I asked of the Lord,
    that will I seek after:
that I may dwell in the house of the Lord
    all the days of my life,
to gaze upon the beauty of the Lord
    and to inquire in his temple.
For he will hide me in his shelter
    in the day of trouble. (vv. 1–5)

Beth and I had a brave goodbye, but tears were near for both of us. Yet she sets out like Paul, who during dark days said to his friends, "What are you doing weeping and breaking my heart? For I am ready not only to be imprisoned but also to die . . . for the name of the Lord Jesus" (Acts 21:13).

# 12

# Incurable Optimism

## Dave and Gloria (Arabian Peninsula)

"God is on a mission. He sent his Son 2,000 years ago to live and to die and to rise again to guarantee its success. It's going forward. And he's invited us to join him—not because we're great, not because we're able, but because our God is."[1]

*Mark Wise, missionary to China*

A few years ago I took a detour from the interstate and caught glimpses of Calvary love on an old battlefield.

### Along the Sunken Road, Fredericksburg, Virginia
*April 8, 2013*

Spent two hours working my way through the parking lot known as I-95 south of Washington, D.C. Took the Fredericksburg exit in search of supper and a bed, but the old battlefield here with its high bluff, known as Marye's Heights, and the Sunken Road at its base have lured me away from the chaos of the afternoon.

Long ago this road left a deep cut through the land, but time has healed the wound. Before me now, the Sunken Road sits in soft dusk, flanked with fresh grass and dandelions. Runners wired with iPods jog alongside a waist-high stone wall, where Confederate soldiers once stood on a frozen morning in December 1862. On that day, this wall bristled with two thousand rifles, awaiting the Union assault. The men in blue had a clear advantage in numbers, but that advantage was soon lost crossing six hundred yards of open ground into a veil of fire. When the smoke cleared, the only thing left was the corpse of a grand army—eight thousand men lay killed or wounded.

As the sun set on that red day, Lee's army held this line, waiting for the next day's battle, and on the other side, Burnside's army awaited their orders. Between them lay a vast, murmuring field of agony. Among the dead, bleeding men cried in pain and intense thirst.

For soldiers on both sides, it was a restless night. The groans of the dying and cries for water broke the silence—and the sleep—of the enemy camps. In the morning, though, no one dared go into this "no-man's-land" to help, for fear of being shot. But Sergeant Richard Kirkland of South Carolina was overcome by these cries and begged his commanding officer that he be allowed to slip over the stone wall to take water to the wounded. His commander finally consented but said that no white flag could be taken—he was on his own.

Kirkland filled all the canteens he could carry and crawled out among his enemies to give them water. As both sides watched, he repeatedly went back, refilling the canteens and returning to wounded men who would come to call him the "Angel of Marye's Heights." On that December morning long ago, there were no doubt hundreds of men on both sides whose hearts broke to hear the cries of their friends and their enemies. I expect that prayers were prayed and noble thoughts thought, but only one man did something about it. Compassion is more than heart. It's also hands and feet—and maybe life, too.

Memorial to the "Angel of Marye's Heights"

Sergeant Kirkland went on to fight at Chancellorsville and Gettysburg, but just ten months after his mission of mercy, he was killed while leading a charge at Chickamauga. He was twenty years old. On his tombstone is inscribed: "If thine enemy thirst, give him drink." These words were spoken by Christ, the Good Samaritan for the world, the one who went to his adversaries, wounded and helpless, and showed matchless mercy. As our cross-bearer, Jesus even took the place of his dying enemies—so that we could live. This is the cost of grace, the radical rescue work of the gospel.

The sun is drawing down, and there is little light left to write by. At the top of Marye's Heights, a bronze general on a pedestal catches the last glint of day. His troops gather around him in perfect formation—row upon row of marble headstones mark the ranks of the unknown dead. The trees are filled with shadows and song, the requiem of the thrush and the mourning dove.

———

Kirkland's deed speaks of the kind of radical, risk-taking love that I've seen on quiet display by Christians going to hard places in the Middle East and serving people who in any other context would be considered enemies. The world we know today began on September 11, 2001, and of the nineteen Al-Qaeda hijackers who turned airplanes into weapons of mass destruction, fifteen were from Saudi Arabia, two from the United Arab Emirates, and the others from Egypt and Lebanon.[2] Since the 9/11 attacks, Islamic terror has shattered our sense of security, spawning wars without borders by enemies without faces. Al-Qaeda and its hideous offspring, Islamic State, and all their franchises and copycat killers have spread their terror worldwide. Behind their black flags is a wake of mass murder and rape done in the name of Allah.

Into this world, Christ sends his servants—men and women who were once themselves enemies and strangers to his grace but now, transformed and driven by the gospel (like Sergeant Kirkland), they risk all to go to their enemies with the Water of Life. Unlike the Angel of Marye's Heights, these foot soldiers of the kingdom go out under the command of their captain, armed with his authority over earth and heaven. These quiet heroes follow a long line of servants "who through faith conquered kingdoms, enforced justice, obtained promises, stopped the mouths of lions, quenched the power of fire, escaped the edge of the sword, were made strong out of weakness" (Heb. 11:33–34). Here's the story of two such servants: Dave and Gloria.

## United Arab Emirates
*March 24, 2016*

Arrived in Dubai. Flight delays triggered by terrorist bombings in Europe made for a long night and day to get here. It was a gray, drizzly, London-like day, as rare rain clouds threw a wet blanket over the usually sparkling high-rises. Even the Burj Khalifa, the world's tallest building, with its head stuck in the clouds, seemed knocked down a notch or two.

However, the view was very different the next day. The wind had swept the clouds away from a sapphire sky, and this time my vantage was from the 125th floor of the Burj Khalifa. Eagles could only look up with envy! Below me, Dubai straddled the space between the desert and the sea. This is the crown jewel in the string of emirates that crowd this corner of southern Arabia. What's easy to forget down there in the urban canyons accented with turquoise pools and green palms is easy to see from up here—the city is a shiny veneer, a house on sand. As the architecture soars to ever new and greater heights, the city must always look over its shoulder at Arabian sand that stretches for a thousand miles from here to Mecca.

Over two million call this home, but the vast majority weren't born here. This is a city not only of Arabs, but also of Iranians, Indians, Pakistanis, Filipinos, and dozens of other peoples. For years, Dubai was mostly just an airport to me—my jump-off point to Afghanistan or Iraq or Pakistan—but after I met Dave and Gloria, that all changed. Gloria told me, "You will never stay in a hotel in this city again!" With such hospitality, Dubai is now itself a destination. And so, it's good to be back and spend time with my friends. Their confidence in the gospel is contagious—and so is their love for the people of this city.

I kicked off the day at Dave and Gloria's Bed and Breakfast with a little coffee and coffee cake. Gloria, always thoughtful, even brought out my favorite coffee mug. Emblazoned with "Don't mess with Texas," it's a feisty reminder of where Dave and Gloria met and married, which was thirteen years, three countries (not counting Texas), and four children ago. Aliza, the oldest, came with them to Arabia, and the other three were born here. Gloria calls them her "desert babies." As is their custom, amid the morning rush to finish breakfast and get off to school, Dave reads the Word and then connects the promises of God with the day ahead. To rephrase Solomon, there's a time for meditation and a time for motion—and Dave does his best to combine the two at breakfast! Afterwards, there was a flurry of shoes, backpacks, and lunch boxes—and I was off with them for the drive to school. Gloria wrote a book titled *Treasuring Christ When Your Hands Are Full*. I can see she has a lot of experience with both treasuring and juggling.

Gloria and I had a good chat on the drive to school and through the morning rush. She has never gotten over the day as a college student when she heard and believed the gospel—and everything changed for her, like being born a second time! Amazing grace is still quite amazing to her. It is the irrevocable promise of God's presence with his people that causes Gloria to be, in her words, "incurably optimistic" that God will bring people in her path to whom she can speak the gospel—at school, at the grocers, or at the mall, where she practices "intentional loitering" in order to talk with someone who needs Jesus. Even at home. She told me that not long ago they had a church pot-luck at their house. The next day a neighbor told her, "All night I had my face glued to my window looking at your yard. I saw Indians and Africans and Asians and Westerners coming together—bringing food and eating at your house and everyone looked so happy. What would bring you all together? Why would you eat with people who are so different from you?"[3] Gloria replied, "Because of Jesus"—and then she shared the gospel with her curious neighbor. Gloria's life is prism-like, as the light of Christ is scattered in beauty wherever she goes.

Gloria

We went on to meet Dave for coffee and to talk over plans for the upcoming Good Friday and Easter services at the church Dave pastors in downtown Dubai. They planted the church seven years ago. They had always wanted to go to a so-called "closed country" but had no clear idea where. Dave and Gloria's "call" to plant a church in the Arabian Peninsula was a literal call—a phone call from a friend who described the spiritual needs and opportunities in Dubai and mentioned there was a lack of healthy churches in the heart of one of the fastest-growing cities in the Middle East. Gloria was listening in on Dave's conversation and went straight to the closet, pulled down her suitcase, tossed in some clothes and her John Piper books, and said, "Let's go!" The two of them still get a good laugh out of Gloria's unhesitating and dramatic response to the moment a door into the unknown was opened and the only guarantees were the ones Christ had given to them in his Word. A readiness to risk and an eagerness to act still characterize their lives and ministries.

This evening we went to Dubai Creek which, for a city not given to understatement, is *some creek*! The wide, saltwater inlet was bustling with boats—from the bulky *dhows*, which look like old pirate ships and are laden with fruits and vegetables from Iran or Oman, to the *abra*, the little sea taxis that shuttle and sputter across the creek constantly. We took an *abra* out in search of supper on the other side. The westward sun was winking on every wave, and the breeze felt good. Found a restaurant on the farther shore, where the golden hour continued to unfold over platters of Arab delights: grilled quail, skewers of lamb, and wedges of flatbread to mop up hummus and *moutabel*, a delicious, smoky eggplant spread.

We talked more about Dave and Gloria's journey. They first met in an Evangelism Explosion class held at their church in Texas, but it was a strange providence that actually brought them together. During a volunteer stint with Habitat for Humanity, a coworker accidentally shot a nail that went through Gloria's right eye. It was a miracle her eye was saved, and it was Gloria's first big test in believing in her God's sovereign control and steadfast love in all things, especially hard situations filled with pain and no easy answers. It was her first big test—but not the last, nor the hardest one.

Dave volunteered to drive Gloria to her numerous doctor's appointments, and eventually Gloria's good Samaritan became her husband! Three years after they were married, though, Dave developed an incurable, degenerative disease known as Reflex Sympathetic Dystrophy. Multiple surgeries have left long scars in his arms but no relief from a disease that has atrophied the muscles in his arms and hands and left him with constant pain—screaming pain—as if his arms are on fire. In addition, he's lost much of the use of his hands. In college Dave played football with friends and held black belts in both karate and Taekwondo, but now many of the simplest tasks are impossible for him—turning a doorknob, brushing his teeth, picking up his little ones. The children help their dad where they can, but much of the care naturally falls to Gloria.

Undeterred, Dave and Gloria came to the Middle East to learn Arabic and plant a church; but before long, everything came to a head—the pain, the humiliation, Gloria's heavy, daily burden to care for her husband and her family, as well as the pressure of all the expectations and appearances of spiritual leadership. Their mission and their marriage were crashing. Dave said that he was not only disabled but also deeply depressed. They came so close to leaving, but in that time of despair, a friend reminded them, "God did not bring you here to destroy you."

What followed was a time of rediscovering the gospel, repentance, and the consequent grace and joy. The Lord did not give Dave and Gloria pain-free days, but he gave them more of himself. He didn't give Dave the use of his hands again, but Jesus showed them his wounded hands instead. As the hymnwriter said, "When through fiery trials thy pathway shall lie, my grace, all-sufficient, shall be thy supply. The flames shall not hurt thee; my only design, thy dross to consume, and thy gold to refine."[4] In this daily suffering, Dave and Gloria are knowing the fellowship of his sufferings and becoming more like their cross-bearer until they see him face to face. And so, for the joy set before them, they are despising the shame and running hard after Christ. These two live and serve in weakness and humility, and for everything that's accomplished—whether planting a church or putting his shoes on—God gets all the glory.

## Dubai

### *Good Friday 2016*

Set out this morning for the church where Dave pastors. A short taxi ride across the neighborhood took us to the hotel where believers were gathering to worship. This is a special morning as we remember our Lord's sacrifice. Prayed with Dave for blessing and help in opening the Word to us this morning, and soon the hotel ballroom filled up for the Good Friday service. A thousand or more people from seventy nations gathered. The worship team was as diverse as the congregation, with an Australian at the keyboard, a Kenyan on the *jembe*, along with several Indians and Filipinos. The church is multi-ethnic but not multicultural. There is one gospel culture here, where people of many nations sing the Word, pray the Word, hear the Word, see the Word, and speak the Word. There was no dumbed-down doctrine—just the unashamed singing and preaching of Christ and him crucified! And so Dave proclaimed the good news of Good Friday! Afterwards, as sons and daughters, we took our place at the Table—remembering with grateful, joyful sorrow, the One who was torn and his life blood poured out to make atonement for the sins of many—to make atonement for me.

## Fujairah
### *Saturday, March 26, 2016*
The clash of cultures comes in many forms. This morning it came with the clatter of diner plates and coffee mugs at the first Denny's that recently opened in the Middle East. A Grand Slam (minus the bacon) in Arabia? However, a stack of pancakes drenched with maple syrup helped me quickly recover from the culture shock!

I joined Dave and his colleague Scott for their Saturday morning Bible study with a group of men they are mentoring—one man is from Hong Kong, another from Kenya, still another from the Philippines, and one from the Bible Belt of the United States! These are future elders and church planters. Besides sharing in the Word, they also read through books together and talk them out. But this is no Saturday morning breakfast club—multiplication is the goal. After a year, each of these men will go on to mentor other men.

Afterwards, Alvin, a Filipino brother, drove Dave and me to Fujairah, a distant emirate on the Indian Ocean side of the peninsula, where there's a church plant underway. As we drove out of Dubai, Alvin pointed out a burned-out building. He told me that four months ago it was home to about five hundred Filipinos who were here for work. A blaze ripped through the building at night, sending hundreds out into the streets with nothing but the clothes on their backs. Gloria heard of the tragedy on the news and was out there first thing in the morning with words of comfort and boxes of doughnuts. Alvin came to see what he could do to help his fellow Filipinos. That day he used his van to transport the now-homeless Filipinos to temporary shelter. With the help of the church, he also brought food, mattresses, and blankets. "Why are you doing this?" they asked. "We are recipients of grace," he answered, "and so we give grace."

But Alvin also told them, "God saved you from this fire, but there is another fire—the fire of his eternal wrath and hell. God has made a way for you to be saved from that fire as well." There's nothing subtle about Alvin's approach, but then there was nothing subtle about Jesus's approach, either, when he said, "Unless you repent, you will all likewise perish" (Luke 13:3). Many of these Filipinos heard and received the gospel, and Alvin is now leading three Bible studies with them.

Took the road east through the desert to Fujairah. This is the "empty quarter." Beyond Sharjah, stopped for a stretch break and a closer look. The Empty Quarter is a fitting name for this vast desert of southern Arabia. Its boundless barrenness is broken by a few moon-like crags. The mountains seem to be sinking into a sea of sand at high tide, while a blazing sun turned up the oven.

Arrived in Fujairah early afternoon and went on to Al Tarboush, a restaurant where we met up with Steve and Akeem, a Pakistani brother Steve is discipling. Steve interned with Dave in Dubai a few years ago. He's planted a church here in this city and is scattering gospel seed up and down the coast. Steve is a steady, courageous, optimistic brother. Perhaps his years of playing football taught him how to brush aside hits, keep moving forward, and keep his eyes on the goal—in this case, magnifying Christ and making disciples who can make disciples.

After the meal, we spread out a map, and Steve pointed out where new small groups were already forming—the nucleus of new church plants. Steve takes the long view—though he's young, he's "old school"—to stay and preach the gospel here for thirty or forty years and multiply himself in men like Akeem, who will start churches that will start churches—both here and in Pakistan. I thought of the word of the Lord in Isaiah where he said, "See, I am doing a new thing! Now it springs up; do you not perceive it? I am making a way in the wilderness and streams in the desert" (Isa. 43:19).

We spent the afternoon together, and it was good to hear more of Steve's confident vision for the work of the gospel in this distant outpost of Christ's kingdom. He and his wife and children have been here for eight years. They've endured, they've suffered, and they've seen new life push up through hard ground. They are the heirs of Samuel Zwemer and other gospel pioneers who came to Arabia, not counting their lives dear unto themselves. Steve likes to quote from Zwemer's writings, as do I. Being with him and with Dave in the epicenter of Islam reminds me of lines Zwemer once penned from these lands: "It was the bigness of the task and its difficulty that thrilled the early Church. Its apparent impossibility was its glory, its worldwide character, its grandeur."[5]

The day was drawing down. We huddled for prayer before parting ways. Dave prayed that this coast "be littered with corporate displays of God's glory." And he prayed for celebrations of the resurrection that will take place here and across southern Arabia in just a few hours, when the sun rises in the east.

## On the Persian Gulf
### *Easter Sunday 2016*

Gathered in the dark before dawn. The moon was setting over the Persian Gulf, and the tints of first light touched the sky beyond the Burj Khalifa. Eventually, some five hundred gathered—many to rejoice in the gospel but some to hear it for the first time. They come from many nations across the region—from Arabia to Pakistan!

Sunrise service: Dave preaching the resurrection

Much of the Christian world regards this region as "closed" and "impossible." But that's not true because Jesus really is alive and is gathering his people from every nation. I saw many of them this morning. Zwemer said it well: "In the struggle for supremacy between Islam and Christianity, the statistics are all on the side of the Muslim, but the dynamics are with the Christian. To those who believe the promises of God, who know the living Christ. . . . We have on our side all the undiscovered wealth of God and his omnipotence."[6]

There is always both excitement and concern about people coming who have never heard the good news of the gospel; so men and women from the church are positioned in the back to greet the newcomers and welcome them into our meeting. They are also there to calm any opponents with kindness and answers. Gloria made a good point on the drive over this morning that Christ has all authority and no underling authority can act apart from his authority; so no man or woman is capable to lift a finger against the King's children apart from his sovereign rule and grace. So what's there to fear?

Between the sea and a mosque, we worshiped Jesus. With a strong voice, Dave preached Christ crucified and risen again and declared how this changes everything! We were filled with such joy and courage to be there together. I thought of George Herbert's words: "Rise heart; Thy Lord is risen. Sing His praise without delays."[7] And so we did, anticipating our own rising:

> Soar we now where Christ hath led, Alleluia!
> Foll'wing our exalted Head, Alleluia!
> Made like him, like him we rise, Alleluia!
> Ours the cross, the grave, the skies, Alleluia![8]

On this special day, the first day, the day of days, the kingdom choir started in the Pacific Islands and the Far East, then across Asia, even rising from prison cells in Iran just across the water. We took up the praise in this corner of Arabia, and before our echoes of "he is risen!" died down, the stanza continued across Africa and Europe, only to be answered from across the Atlantic with "he is risen indeed!"

## Dohuk, Iraq
### August 30, 2017

Dave and I departed Dubai dark and early this morning on a three-hour flight to Erbil. We've been talking about making this trip for more than a year; so it's good to finally do it. Dave has former church members who are serving in Iraq, and I think it's pretty hard-core of him to fly to a war zone to counsel and encourage them. I know others at his church are considering coming, as well. Dave's church has a "revolving door" in the best sense because they are making and sending disciples, and so he wants to scout out the opportunities firsthand. His pain and physical limitations are great, but his spirit is irrepressible, and his pastor's heart beats for his people. I only hope I can do a good job accompanying him and be tuned in to anticipate what he needs so that as much as possible he won't even have to ask for help. We'll be a team!

Iraq is every shade of brown this time of year—in contrast to when I was last here in the spring, when the land was washed with green. After breezing through passport control, we went over to Mack and Leeann's apartment for breakfast. Mack was an elder at Dave's church in Dubai, and they are recent arrivals in Kurdistan, where Mack has taken the pastorate of an international church in Erbil. We were refreshed by their hospitality and the stories of grace we shared around the table.

Afterwards, Dave and I set out for Dohuk to catch up with friends. The drive is little more than two hours now that the front lines have shifted and there are fewer checkpoints. I sense something different in the air since I was here last. Nearby, Mosul has been retaken from Islamic State, and the Kurds are justifiably proud of the decisive role they have had in the terrible war against ISIS, but there is little cheering—just sad resignation that peace is just a prelude to more war with one or more of the enemies that crouch at their borders.

## Erbil, Iraq
### *September 1, 2017*
Returned to Erbil last night and met up for coffee this morning with Matt and Betsy, who are serving with different aid organizations. Betsy's group provides shelter and food for the thousands

of refugees that continue to pour out of this wounded land, and Matt is helping provide prosthetics and wheelchairs for those who are in the most desperate need. In even the hardest places, Jesus has positioned his servants. Their hands—like his—are open, comforting, blistered, and stained.

This afternoon Dave preached at the international church from Psalm 42. It was good to hear him preach once more before we part ways tomorrow. The message walked through the psalm with all its hurt and hope. The psalmist's struggles echoed Dave's own, and so Dave preached from his pain to us in our own brokenness.

> As a deer pants for flowing streams,
>     so pants my soul for you, O God.
> My soul thirsts for God,
>     for the living God.
> When shall I come and appear before God?
> My tears have been my food
>     day and night,
> while they say to me all the day long,
>     "Where is your God?" . . .
> I say to God, my rock: "Why have you forgotten me?
>     Why do I go mourning
> because of the oppression of the enemy?"
>     As with a deadly wound in my bones,
> my adversaries taunt me,
>     while they say to me all the day long,
> "Where is your God?"
>     Why are you cast down, O my soul,
> and why are you in turmoil within me?
>     Hope in God; for I shall again praise him,
>         my salvation and my God. (Ps. 42:1–3, 9–11)

Dave spoke honestly about pain and depression both from the Bible and from his own experience, but he also pointed us to

Jesus and went on to tell of God's radical rescue mission in all its beauty and cross-centered power.

Seeing and hearing Dave preach through his deep pain with joyful confidence reminds me that "God chose what is weak in the world to shame the strong; God chose what is low and despised in the world, even things that are not, to bring to nothing things that are, so that no human being might boast in the presence of God" (1 Cor. 1:27–29). It's a sweet providence that all I'm seeing and hearing today is unfolding in Iraq because this is Hebrews 11 country. This is the same land where centuries ago Daniel by faith "stopped the mouths of lions" and here by faith his friends Shadrach, Meshach, and Abednego faced the furnace for their unbending testimony that there is only one true and living God. The Son of Man, the fourth man in the flames with them, "quenched the power of fire" (Heb. 11:33–34).

Christ still walks with his people in the fire. I've seen this reality on display in Dave and Gloria, as well as in my other brothers and sisters across these desert lands. They serve in pain and joy, heartache and hope, speaking words of life in the very face of death and deep darkness. They press ahead, knowing that "as grace extends to more and more people it may increase thanksgiving, to the glory of God. So we do not lose heart. Though our outer self is wasting away, our inner self is being renewed day by day. For this light momentary affliction is preparing for us an eternal weight of glory beyond all comparison" (2 Cor. 4:15–17).

# 13

# "He Showed Them His Hands"

## Jakob (Syria and Armenia)

"Those who have once seen the scars of Jesus can never live the old life again. He never hid His scars to win disciples. He showed them. They proved His victory, and are the badge of His eternal authority."[1]

*Samuel Zwemer*

"I see mercy in Your hands."[2]

*Bob Kauflin*

Scars tell stories. They may be stories as routine as shoulder surgery. Or scars may tell of selfless love, such as those left by burns received by rescuing a child from a fire. Or they may be marks of desperate courage received on a battlefield. My uncle's arms were disfigured by wounds received in hand-to-hand combat in World War II. Despite being outnumbered and outgunned, he fought valiantly; but in the end, he was struck with three bullets that left gaping wounds. He should have died that day (and his enemies believed he was dead), but God was in control even when everything suddenly seemed out of control.

Harry Wright in 2011 and 1944

The scars Harry Wright carried for the rest of his life were reminders of sacrifice and survival but also, in a strange way, marks of sovereign grace. Until the day he died at the age of ninety-two, he gave glory to Christ, the one who saved him twice—on the battlefield and for all eternity. The humility that characterized his life was rooted in the gift that each day was for him. And there was no boasting—except in Jesus.

And Jesus also has scars.

As the day of Jesus's resurrection drew to a close, his disciples were in a state of confusion. That morning, breathless reports came from some of the women that the tomb was empty and that Mary Magdalene had seen Jesus alive, and by early evening, a similar report came from the village of Emmaus, seven miles away. That morning after hearing the news, Peter and John ran to the tomb and could confirm that it was empty. But what did it mean? There had been a lot of running around that day with little to show for it except they were footsore and fearful as night settled over Jerusalem. The heady days of palm branches and hosannas just a week earlier seemed like a lifetime ago. Nighttime was just another reminder of dark Gethsemane, the night they ran for their lives and not one of them kept their word that they would never forsake their master. In their shame, guilt, and confusion, they were hiding from their past and fearing their future. But all that was about to change.

"On the evening of that day, the first day of the week, the doors being locked where the disciples were for fear of the Jews, Jesus came and stood among them and said to them, 'Peace be with you.' When he had said this, he showed them his hands and his side. Then the disciples were glad when they saw the Lord. Jesus said to them again, 'Peace be with you. As the Father has sent me, even so I am sending you'" (John 20:19–21).

Tim Keller wrote,

> When Jesus shows the disciples his hands and feet, he is showing them his scars. The last time the disciples saw Jesus, they thought those scars were ruining their lives. The disciples had thought they were on a presidential campaign. They thought their candidate was going to win and they were going to be in the cabinet, and when they saw the nails going into the hands and the feet and the spear going into the side, they believed those wounds had destroyed their lives. And now Jesus is showing them that in his resurrected body his scars are still there.
>
> Why is this important? Because now that they understand the scars, the sight and memory of them will increase the glory and joy of the rest of their lives. Seeing Jesus Christ with his scars, reminds them of what he did for them—that

the scars they thought had ruined their lives actually saved their lives. Remembering those scars will help many of them endure their own crucifixions.[3]

The disciples recognized Jesus by the scars in his hands. It was a gift of grace that these remained in his glorified, resurrected body so that one day, like the first disciples, we, too, will recognize our risen King by the marks of Calvary love. Jesus's scars not only show his triumph over death but are the seal of his authority over heaven and over all the earth, to which he sends his gospel messengers. Abraham Kuyper famously said, "There is not a square inch in the whole domain of our human existence over which Christ, who is Sovereign over all, does not cry: 'Mine!'"[4]

Christ is in charge of all things—every inch and every second. The global reach of the every-tribe-every-tongue gospel has the print of the nails upon it in both the salvation and the suffering of Christ's own. I was reminded of that in vivid ways when I traveled to the land of Noah on the plains of Ararat.

### In Flight, Moscow to Yerevan, Armenia
*July 18, 2017*

It's been a turbulent flight since leaving Moscow—a five-hundred-mile-an-hour roller coaster ride, enough to keep me awake after a twenty-four-hour whirlwind that began in Brooklyn and will end in Armenia. Yesterday about this time I was walking the streets of Brooklyn. The noon-high sun shimmered on the traffic that slithered down Flatbush through a crowded canyon under perpetual construction. Crossed Flatbush and made my way to the only green spot in view—Fort Greene Park—a splendid, tree-covered hill where I could catch a few precious minutes with my son. Tim often comes here on his lunch break since his architectural company is only about a mile away. Like me, he likes to walk—and walk fast. Tim was waiting at the top, and we munched on sandwiches and talked until we both had to go, which was painfully quick. As he walked back down the long, green slope to the Brooklyn Navy Yard, I watched until he disappeared into the crowds below. My heart followed him in love and pride and prayer for my son—a man now making his own way in the world.

Caught a taxi to JFK airport for a rendezvous with Craig Baxter, a pastor friend in New Jersey who will be my guide to Armenia over the next few days. Made good time getting to JFK. The way the cabbie drove, I could easily imagine that he was a retired Hollywood stunt driver or had recently robbed a bank! After I reached JFK to meet Craig and catch our flight, Craig called to let me know he had forgotten his passport and was returning to retrieve it. I was afraid this was going to scuttle our departure plans, but amazingly Craig made it back in time! After we cleared security, I saw sovereign purpose and perfect timing in all the delays—a forgotten passport, the rush-hour traffic, and the belligerent TSA officer, who slowed us down even more. As we reached our gate area, Craig had a "chance" meeting with a Jewish man named Obadiah.

Craig and Obadiah quickly struck up a meaningful conversation because Obadiah is a man of peace (in the Luke 10 sense)—open, thoughtful—and Craig is a Spirit-enabled messenger (also in the Luke 10 sense). Obadiah said he was searching for the truth and had moved to Israel in an effort to find it. "Did you find truth there?" Craig asked. Obadiah said he did because now he could speak to God and had a relationship with him—a relationship based on his obedience to God's commands. When Craig gently pressed on that point, Obadiah admitted he fell short. He understood repentance was more than "being sorry" for sin and that it requires justice. The sacrifices under Moses provided the satisfaction that was needed, but the temple was gone and he awaited the Messiah, the King who would bring justice and set things right. Craig then opened the Scripture to Isaiah 53 and read, "Surely he has borne our griefs and carried our sorrows; yet we esteemed him stricken, smitten by God, and afflicted. But he was pierced for our transgressions; he was crushed for our iniquities; upon him was the chastisement that brought us peace, and with his wounds we are healed" (v. 5). My jaw dropped when Obadiah said, "Who is this speaking of?" I thought of the Ethiopian's same question in Acts 8. And like Philip the evangelist, Craig the evangelist "beginning with this Scripture he told him the good news about Jesus" (Acts 8:35).

We were starting to board our flight and had to part ways, but Obadiah gave Craig his contact information and invited followup. Craig's forgotten passport was a sovereign delay ordering his steps and seconds to be able to speak clearly of Christ, the Messiah who has already come and who through his cross-work is himself our justice, satisfaction, and righteousness.

Flew on to Moscow, where Craig and I grabbed a wake-up cup to shake off the short night. Then we boarded this Aeroflot flight to Yerevan. The turbulence has passed for now. Craig is working through a sheath of notes, and I am catching up on my journal. Craig has deep ties to a number of pastors in Armenia and will be preaching at a conference for them. For my part, I especially want to meet one of them—a Syrian pastor named Jakob, a refugee from Aleppo who is pastoring a congregation of refugees from Aleppo. I want to hear his story.

We're on approach now to the Armenian capital. Despite the dusky orange skies, there is still enough light left to trace the face of mighty Ararat.

### Tsakhkadzor, Armenia
**July 20, 2017**

Yesterday drove north from Yerevan to this picturesque town with a few too many consonants in its name. The meaning of "Tsakhkadzor" is as beautiful as the view—and much easier to pronounce. Since ancient times it's been called "Valley of Flowers."

The conference Craig was preparing for is being held here. Nearly one hundred pastors have gathered from across Armenia. It's good to see both gray heads and young men—men in their twenties up to those in their seventies. The highlight has been hearing them sing, as the sound of a hundred brothers joined their strong, deep voices and filled this place with great praise!

Between sessions, I have enjoyed hearing their stories of saving grace and gospel power. One brother, Norik, is a joy-filled evangelist. He went to prison six times—not for his gospel work but because of serious crimes he had committed. Norik was finally sent to a maximum security prison in Omsk, Russia. One day a Christian visiting the prison gave Norik a New Testament and said, "This is God's message to you. If you read it and ask him, he will speak to you through it." In Matthew's Gospel, Norik met Jesus—the one who lived and died and rose again to "save his people from their sins." Norik believed and was radically changed—like being born a second time! Norik was discipled by a pastor who visited the prison, and soon Norik was sharing his good news with his fellow prisoners—and many believed on the Lord Jesus. Before long, a church of redeemed prisoners formed inside the walls and razor wire! After Norik's release a few years ago, he returned to his native Armenia and continues to share the gospel that sets prisoners free, delivering them from sin, death, and deep darkness.

Afterwards, I was able to meet Jakob to hear his story. Jakob and his family are from Aleppo—the once great city in Syria that is now a great grave. Beginning in 2012, Aleppo endured a four-year-long siege by Syrian government forces and their Russian allies against an array of rebel groups. It was the longest siege in modern warfare. It is Syria's Stalingrad. Thirty-one thousand died, and untold thousands more were maimed—from the Syrian and Russian air forces using barrel bombs and chemical weapons. Most of the casualties were civilians caught in the middle. Besides all this, an assortment of armies, militias, and mercenaries inside and outside Aleppo slugged it out—some even switched sides in the middle of the fight. And the city became a vast killing field of bloodshed and betrayal. I recall how one war correspondent in Aleppo described the relentless, senseless killing.

The regime forces, led by President Bashar al-Assad, use barrel bombs—a type of improvised explosive device (IED). The bombs are like no other I have witnessed in the dozen or more wars I have lived through. They are unspeakably effective at causing pain: made from a barrel that is filled with shrapnel or chemicals, they are then dropped from a height by helicopter or aeroplane. Militants like them because they are cheap to make (sometimes costing under $300) and can easily be dropped on a highly populated civilian area, with severe consequences.

The image of the aftermath of a barrel bomb: knee-deep rubble, cries of agony, the frantic search for survivors; limbs dissected, muscles and pools of sticky blood. The fact of being alive in concrete, rubble, your legs broken, waiting for someone to dig you out. The entire weight of an apartment floor crushing your suddenly helpless and broken body.[5]

In the midst of this hell, Jakob pastored two congregations. One was a Syrian church where several hundred Christians of mostly Armenian descent worshiped. In another district of Aleppo, Jakob pastored a Kurdish congregation—men and women he had led to Christ out of Islam. It was dangerous work sharing the gospel with Muslims and discipling new believers among them, but God prospered the work and the congregation grew to about a hundred.

One evening several months into the siege, Jakob and his wife stepped out onto the balcony of their apartment during a lull in the fighting. Suddenly, a distant sniper's bullet struck. His wife was shot in the leg just above the knee. In that split second, Jakob instinctively raised his arms and the second bullet struck his left hand, stopping the bullet from hitting his heart. They were taken to a makeshift hospital. Miraculously, his wife's wound was clean. The bullet just missed her knee and main artery. For Jakob, the bullet penetrated the side of his hand and stopped in the middle. With only local anesthetic, the doctor cut the bullet out and sewed up his hand. I asked Jakob if he would show me his hand. An ugly scar gouged the side where the bullet entered, and he had another scar in the middle of his hand where the bullet was extracted.

After this, Jakob and his family remained in Aleppo to shepherd the flock, though many of the Christians were fleeing to Armenia as refugees. Jakob said the fighting cut him off from the Kurdish believers, which was a deep sorrow to him, and eventually those Christians were all killed or scattered. More than a year after being struck by the sniper, a rocket destroyed their apartment building. Jakob, his wife, and their children climbed out of the rubble and moved to a temporary shelter. By this time most of the members of his church had fled to Armenia, and these refugees pleaded for their pastor to come there, too, and shepherd them. After wrestling with God over this hard decision, Jakob was eventually given peace to go. So, he and his family took the last escape route still open out of the city.

Jakob has been in Armenia for two years now—a refugee pastoring refugees. He described the challenges for his people. There are problems of pain and loss, to be sure, but there are also challenges of how to reach the city they have now fled to. Jakob kindly invited me to join them on Sunday.

The hour was late, and Jakob had been so patient to answer my questions, but I had one final one for him. I quoted Philippians 3:10: "That I may know him, and the power of his resurrection, and the fellowship of his sufferings" (KJV). I asked Jakob in what ways he has known Christ more in the fellowship of his sufferings. Jakob said he knows the reality that Christ is standing near to him *every second*. Of the constant pain in his hand and the scars that trace his wound, Jakob said, "In my pain I feel his pain. In his blessing I feel his mercy."

## Khor Virap, Armenia, on the Plains of Ararat
### July 22, 2017

Set out early this morning before the sun and heat rose higher. Temperatures most days this week in Yerevan have been in the hundreds or more. So we raced the sun westward to Khor Virap. Our road cut through a rich land. Huddled along the wayside were produce stands stuffed with corn and watermelons, tomatoes, apples, and apricots, which were just coming in. I saw many orchards specked with these dull orange delights. Well-manicured vineyards stretched out in neat rows to a western horizon dominated by Mount Ararat, towering over all and still sporting its winter cap in late July. This mountain is a magnificent, timeless witness to the unfolding story of redemption.

Mount Ararat from Khor Virap

Reached Khor Virap, an ancient church that crowns a little stone prominence rising above the plains but dwarfed by nearby Ararat. At the foot of Khor Virap is the Armenian-Turkish border, sharply defined with razor wire and accented with guard towers. All the land in view, including Noah's mighty mountain, was for centuries the homeland of the Armenian people. Caught between its powerful, ravenous neighbors—Turkey, Persia, and Russia—their lands were absorbed, culminating in the twentieth century's first genocide. Sadly, it would be only the first chapter in a century-long chronicle of evil filled with the gas chambers of Auschwitz, the chilling images of tortured children at Tuol Sleng, and all the shallow graves that stain the faces of Bosnia, Kosovo, Rwanda, Syria, and Iraq.

Mass killings of Armenians by the Turks had been so common as to be something of a national pastime by the late nineteenth century, but the bloodiest blow would come in 1915. At that time, murder and mass deportation were carried out by the Ottoman Turks against their Armenian citizens. More than a million died in this genocide, and hundreds of thousands fled this terror, finding refuge across the border into Syria as well as migrating to Europe and America. Jakob and the other Armenians from Aleppo are the children and grandchildren of the victims of the genocide. A century later, like a recurring nightmare, the Syrian bloodletting has made them refugees, too.

Several olive trees cling to the stony slopes of Khor Virap. I plucked some olive leaves, recalling the passage in Genesis where Noah "sent forth the dove out of the ark. And the dove came back to him in the evening, and behold, in her mouth was a freshly plucked olive leaf. So Noah knew that the waters had subsided from the earth" (Gen. 8:10–11).

While these olive leaves were a beautiful symbol of peace for Noah, these lands have never known peace since then. The razor-wire lined border that is just a stone's throw from where I sit is one more witness to that fact. Christ is the only one who can take the children of Cain and cleanse their hearts and hands and give them peace with God and peace with each other.

For Jakob and my other brothers and sisters who have suffered so much in the war, this peace is the one thing that lasts when all else has been torn from their arms. The peace that men make is as fragile as those who make it. But the peace of Christ is made on "better promises" and comes with his comfort, for with nail-scarred hands he will also wipe all tears from our eyes.

### Yerevan, Armenia
*Sunday, July 23, 2017*

Refugee church, Pastor Jakob in the foreground

Worshiped with a congregation of Syrian refugees from Aleppo. Pastor Jakob spoke as a pilgrim to pilgrims when he declared that like Abraham by faith they all seek "a better country" (Heb. 11:16). I believe these Christians see that land more clearly than I do. Their tears and their scars are real, but their joy is real, too. Fervent prayer and joyful singing filled the place. A sister named

Noushik played the keyboard. She could rip the keys with one hand and point heavenward with the other! They sang:

Worthy, worthy, worthy, to receive honor.
You are awesome, God of power, Lord of glory.
Come and fill this place.

The joy of these believers is certainly not because of their circumstances, but it is in and through the God who raises the dead.

Afterwards Craig and I went out to lunch with Jakob and his family. Jakob would not let us pay. He kindly, firmly insisted and said with a smile, "Heaven will provide." Our fellowship this afternoon was sweet, and I told him how much it meant to me to share in the joy of worship this morning. Jakob said, "For years I sowed seed in Syria that I am now harvesting in Armenia." There are thousands of Armenian-Syrian refugees in Yerevan. They've shared the trail of tears that brought them here, and now the church will show by witness and acts of mercy the path that will truly and finally bring them home.

# 14

# Things as They Are

## Amy Carmichael and William Carey (India)

"The work of a true missionary is work indeed, often very monotonous, apparently not very successful, and carried on through great and varied but unceasing difficulties."[1]

*Hudson Taylor*

In the 1890s a missionary society in England asked the intrepid Amy Carmichael to write a book about her gospel work in India. Such a book would help engage more churches and inspire and mobilize more women and men to go and serve Christ in the vast, neglected field of India. A gifted writer, Amy told of the heavy layers of darkness that hung over the people because of Hinduism and caste. She described the horrors of the sexual exploitation of children on a grand scale by the temple priests. "Talk of beasts in human shape!" she said. "It is slandering good animals to compare bad men to beasts."[2] "We are skirting the abyss, an abyss which is deep and foul beyond description, and yet is glorified, to Hindu eyes, by the sanctions of religion."[3]

The missionary society returned the manuscript to Carmichael. Couldn't she tell better stories? Couldn't she show more numbers and results? It would be hard to raise funds and workers with such a depressing book.

Amy Carmichael

Amy put the manuscript away and went about her work.

Sometime later, friends from England were visiting Amy and heard about the rejected manuscript. They asked if they could take it back to England and find a publisher. The result was the 1903 publication of *Things As They Are*—a fitting title and a fitting rebuke. This book is filled with details and photographs of life and ministry in southern India, but it's really a story about the radical rescue work of the gospel on the edge of "an abyss." Therefore, it speaks to the challenges of pioneer missions then and now—and everywhere. This book also contains one of the most vivid, haunting, and convicting passages in all of missionary literature. One night, as temple drums beat on, Amy opened a window into the darkness—and drew us up with her to see and hear, too.

The tom-toms thumped straight on all night, and the darkness shuddered round me like a living, feeling thing. I could not go to sleep, so I lay awake and looked; and I saw, as it seemed, this:

That I stood on a grassy sward, and at my feet a precipice broke sheer down into infinite space. I looked, but saw no bottom; only cloud shapes, black and furiously coiled, and great shadow-shrouded hollows, and unfathomable depths. Back I drew, dizzy at the depth.

Then I saw forms of people moving single file along the grass. They were making for the edge. There was a woman with a baby in her arms and another little child holding on to her dress. She was on the very verge. Then I saw that she was blind. She lifted her foot for the next step . . . it trod air. She was over, and the children with her. Oh, the cry as they went over!

Then I saw more streams of people flowing from all quarters. All were blind, stone blind; all made straight for the precipice edge. There were shrieks as they suddenly knew themselves falling, and a tossing up of helpless arms, catching, clutching at empty air. But some went over quietly, and fell without a sound.

Then I wondered, with a wonder that was simply agony, why no one stopped them at the edge. I could not. I was glued to the ground, and I could not call; though I strained and tried, only a whisper would come out.

Then I saw that along the edge there were sentries set at intervals. But the intervals were far too great; there were wide, unguarded gaps between. And over these gaps the people fell in their blindness, quite unwarned; and the green grass seemed blood-red to me, and the gulf yawned like the mouth of hell.

Then I saw, like a little picture of peace, a group of people under some trees with their backs turned towards the gulf. They were making daisy chains. Sometimes when a piercing shriek cut the quiet air and reached them it disturbed them, and they thought it a rather vulgar noise. And if one of their number started up and wanted to go and do something to help, then all the others would pull that one down. "Why should you get so excited about it? You must wait for a definite call to go! You haven't finished your daisy chains yet. It would be really selfish," they said, "to leave us to finish the work alone."

There was another group. It was made up of people whose great desire was to get more sentries out; but they found that very few wanted to go, and sometimes there were no sentries for miles and miles of the edge.

Once a girl stood alone in her place, waving the people back; but her mother and other relations called, and reminded her that her furlough was due; she must not break the rules. And being tired and needing a change, she had to go and rest for awhile; but no one was sent to guard her gap, and over and over the people fell, like a waterfall of souls.

Once a child caught at a tuft of grass that grew at the very brink of the gulf; it clung convulsively, and it called—but nobody seemed to hear. Then the roots of the grass gave way, and with a cry the child went over, its two little hands still holding tight to the torn-off bunch of grass. And the girl who longed to be back in her gap thought she heard the little one cry, and she sprang up and wanted to go; at which they reproved her, reminding her that no one is necessary any-where; the gap would be well taken care of, they knew. And then they sang a hymn.

Then through the hymn came another sound like the pain of a million broken hearts wrung out in one full drop, one sob. And a horror of great darkness was upon me, for I knew what it was—The Cry of the Blood.

Then thundered a Voice, the Voice of the Lord: "And He said, What hast thou done? The voice of thy brother's blood crieth unto Me from the ground."[4]

No wonder the nice missionary society returned the manuscript.

In her plea for more workers, Amy Carmichael presented not alluring stories but "the truth—the uninteresting, unromantic truth."[5] Her book was not one of despair—far from it. It was a clear-eyed view of the situation on the ground matched with confidence in the cross-centered power of the gospel.

More has been written about the successes than about the failures, and it seems to us that it is more important that you should know about the reverses than about the successes of the war. We shall have all eternity to celebrate the victories, but we have only the few hours before sunset in which to win them. We are not winning them as we should, because the fact of the reverses is so little realised, and the needed reinforcements are not forthcoming, as they would be if the position were thoroughly understood. Reinforcements of men and women are needed, but, far above all, reinforce-ments of prayer. And so we have tried to tell you the truth— the uninteresting, unromantic truth. . . . The work is not a pretty thing, to be looked at and admired. It is a fight. And battlefields are not beautiful.[6]

It's still that way. Not long ago a missionary friend shared his letter to a pastor who asked him how he should present missions in his church. Like *Things As They Are*, the letter rang with the unromantic truth as well as the unbroken grace given to take the unstoppable gospel to the very gates of hell.

Let them know the incredible difficulty of "leaving houses and lands . . ." for the Gospel. It's easy to feel the tingly sensations of missionary surrender by listening to a well-crafted, musically powerful missionary DVD in a climate-controlled auditorium and then hearing an impassioned sermon. But turn off the A/C when you preach the sermon. Pump in the smells of body odor and strange food and cigarette smoke. Talk about depression and loneliness and pain and smog and threats and fears and danger and discomfort. Talk about there being 10 Demases that rip your heart out for every Timothy that is faithful. Talk about pouring out blood, sweat, and tears and seeing the harvest come in slower than you thought it would. Talk about missionary kids struggling to adjust and forever becoming "third-culture" people—neither being culturally American nor Timbuktuan. Missionary sacrifice is overwhelming. This isn't in the fine print—it's plastered all over the New Testament—but we fail to present this side because we don't want to sound like we're bellyaching. War is Hell.

But also let them know the incredible reward of doing all this for Christ's sake. Talk up the "joy" that was set before Christ at the cross. Talk up eternal treasure. Mention the party thrown over the 1-in-100 rescued from destruction. Make them jealous for God's glory and tell them how incredibly amazing it is to see God turn on the spiritual light in a pagan's heart, how tear-jerkingly awesome it is to hear a sinner calling upon the name of the Lord, that, amidst the pagan sounds and oppressive darkness, you have been sent as a light, lit by the Light. You are there, and they know you are there, and *he* knows you are there — and *he* is there with you. Always. Until it's all over and you go to your final sleep saying, "I left it all on out there on the field—and it was worth it all."[7]

Elisabeth Elliot summarized not only Amy Carmichael's work but also her own ministry in Ecuador, where her husband and friends were killed, as well as many other frontiers where the gospel's long campaign is underway, when she wrote, "If it were possible to poll all the missionaries who have worked in all the world in all of Christian history, it would be seen that missionary work, most of the time, offers little that could be called glamour. What it does offer, as Amy wrote to prospective candidates in later years, is 'a chance to die'—or, as Winston Churchill put his challenge during World War II, blood, sweat, and tears. It offers a great deal of plodding and ploughing, with now and then a little planting. It is the promise of rejoicing, given to those who 'go forth weeping, bearing precious seed' that gives heart."[8]

William Carey preceded Amy Carmichael to India by a century. Carey's often-quoted "expect great things from God, attempt great things for God"[9] could well be the ten-word biography of "the morning star of modern missions."[10] These inspirational words were not empty ones for Carey. He was not whistling in the dark, but rather he was stating the facts of faith and the trajectory of his life. However, Carey would also write in his journal:

> Had a miserable Day, sorely harassed from without, and very Cold and dead in my Soul. I could bear all outward trials if I had but more of the spirit of God. . . .
>
> I sometimes walk in my Garden and try to pray to God, and if I pray at all, it is in the Solitude of a Walk; I thought my soul a little drawn out to day, but soon gross darkness returned; spoke a word or two to a Mohammedan upon the things of God, but I feel as bad as they. . . .

O that this day could be consigned to Oblivion, What a mixture of Impatience, carelessness, forgetfulness of God, Pride, and peevishness have I felt this day—God forgive me.[11]

Steady, purposeful, plodding was Carey's greatest strength. In Carey's ministry "things as they are" included both miserable days as well as days when he preached good news to hundreds. There were triumphs of putting the Bible into the languages of millions of people in South Asia and of seeing Indians turn "to God from idols to serve the living and true God" (1 Thess. 1:9). But it also included fires, floods, funerals, persecution, poverty, loneliness, betrayal by friends, and slander by critics.

William Carey
Engraving by John Brown Myers; London 1887

A few years ago, Aashish, an Indian pastor, and I traveled to Serampore, Kolkata, and up the Ganges to Varanasi—all places of significance in Carey's life and legacy. What struck me as I walked along the banks of the Hooghly, the streets of Old Calcutta, and the *ghats* along the Ganges was how little was left to see there of Carey's work. I got a glimpse of things as they were and things as they are. It was a vivid reminder that the influence of a life transformed by the gospel that expects great things and attempts great things is not measured by monuments but by something far more durable—the glory of the risen King. Carey's vision-in-action influenced generations of gospel risk-takers. A great company of heroes—from Adoniram Judson to Amy Carmichael, from Jim and Elisabeth Elliot to missionary pathfinders today—continue, like Carey, to make Jesus famous to the ends of the earth. Near the end of his life, Carey chided a friend about the adulations he had written about the work in India. "You have been saying much about Dr. Carey and his work. When I am gone, say nothing about Dr. Carey; speak about Dr. Carey's Saviour."[12]

## Kolkata, India
### September 8, 2010

Set out for Serampore at first light. Two hundred years ago this was home to Carey and his team. This "father of modern missions" had a vision for worldwide evangelization when few others had a big enough view of God to see it. Carey's example of vision, action, and endurance has meant much to me personally. I can hardly believe I'm here, walking through what were only pages in a book before. Here along the Hooghly River was the center of forty years of Carey's ministry—preaching, teaching, translation work, social reform efforts, and his beloved garden, where he often resorted to for prayer. Today the garden grounds are somewhere under a grimy, belching jute factory that's crowded about with transport trucks. I worked my way past the lorries, climbed through a barbed wire fence, to the littered grounds where I found the cross which marks the spot where, after six long years of persistent ministry, Carey baptized the first Indian convert. Nearby is the college that he started as well as a little museum that holds a few brittle copies of the Bibles he translated.

A mile or so away we found the cemetery where he, his family, and colleagues are buried. Aashish coaxed the caretaker's daughter to open the gate for us. In the corner of the cemetery, Carey's grave is marked by a simple stone and epitaph, words that he chose from an Isaac Watts hymn—"A wretched, poor, and helpless worm, on Thy kind arms I fall."

Sadly, most Indians today have never heard of William Carey or his God. Serampore, like every other Indian town, is stuffed with idols. A century after Carey's death, his college had departed from the faith, embracing liberalism and shunning the message of the gospel that Carey had so faithfully preached. Today it has become just a nice place to go to college. I am left feeling that there should be more to show for such a life; but Carey's monuments aren't made of bricks or marble, but rather something so much bigger. He gave India the Bible. In fact, he gave this polyglot people with its tangle of tongues several Bibles. He translated the entire Bible into six major Indian languages and portions of the Bible into twenty-nine other Asian languages. Carey knew that "the entrance of thy words giveth light" (Ps. 119:130 KJV). In the lineage of Luther and Tyndale, he believed that the best preacher was the Bible in the language of the people. Across India, from Afghanistan to Burma, people can now read and receive the good news in their heart language. *This* is Carey's living legacy.

Afterward returned to Kolkata. Before heading to the train station, stopped at Kumartuli, a tangle of alleys where the idol makers ply their trade. They twist some straw, shape some mud over it, add some paint and sparkles, and voila! "Behold your god!" The Bengalis here are in the midst of the festival of Durga Puja. Durga's ten arms make her look a bit like Spiderwoman. I thought of the words of Jeremiah, "Their idols are like scarecrows in a cucumber field, and they cannot speak; they have to be carried, for they cannot walk. Do not be afraid of them, for they cannot do evil, neither is it in them to do good. . . . There is no breath in them. They are worthless, a work of delusion" (Jer. 10:5, 14–15). The blindness of these people is profound; like their gods, they are born without eyes.

The idol makers could see that my friend Aashish and I were not exactly in awe of the work of their hands. Several young men gathered at one end of the narrow alley and appeared ready for a fight. They made their way toward us and grew in number, and I knew from the story of Demetrius and those Ephesian silversmiths how much trouble angry idol makers can stir up; so Aashish and I mixed in with the crowd and chose another way out. We had a train to catch.

Took the 8:30 train this evening to Varanasi. The rail station in Kolkata is a microcosm of India. The sights, smells, and crowds are all here. The stench of urine and incense hangs in the air over a platform smeared with spit and excrement. Beggars, dogs, the deranged, all mingle with the chaotic crowds that, like me, were rushing to find their train. We've settled in for the night with fifteen hours ahead of us.

### Varanasi, India
*September 9, 2010*

I woke to a vast green sea of rice as our train lurched on toward Varanasi. My train window is a kaleidoscope of life along the rail. In swift sequences, I see a man living under an umbrella, his possessions all under its shadow. There's a one-armed man rushing to catch the train, his sleeve sweeping past him. There are giggling schoolgirls tripping along a dusty road, and in the distant rice fields women in bright saris bend to their tasks, dotting the green void like a string of gems.

Reached Varanasi. Our hired driver here is a gentleman named Somnat—likeable and helpful in getting around the city. He is a devotee of Ganesh, the elephant-headed god. Aashish took the opportunity to share Christ—*Ishu Masih*—with him. Aashish's approach is to ask searching questions, modeled after

Jesus's approach to engaging in gospel conversations. May the Lord give Somnat light to know him.

For much of its three thousand years Varanasi was called Kashi, "city of light." I think nothing could be further from the truth. This is the holiest city of Hinduism, their mecca huddled along the muddy, filthy Ganges, which they worship as a goddess and believe that its waters can wash away sins. For centuries, unwanted children—especially daughters—were "offered" to the goddess Ganges. That is, they were drowned in the river. William Carey was shocked by this widespread infanticide, as he was about *sati*, the burning of widows. Women were tied to the corpse of their husbands and burned alive on the funeral pyre. *Sati* was commonplace across much of India, but here in Varanasi, there was added "blessing" for killing women and children in this place. Carey never stopped campaigning against these horrors. He preached, published, and lobbied for the lives of the most vulnerable of God's image-bearers. His efforts spared many, and eventually these Hindu practices were outlawed.

Walked toward the river and the *ghats*, the steps that descend into it. The streets were filled with holy cows and holy men. The sheer scale of this spectacle seems to give weight to the worship, for there are millions who come here each year to drink this sacred water and to wash away their sins. Those who sit hopelessly scrubbing at their sins in a muddy river do not yet know of grace, of the Lord's awesome work spoken of in Ezekiel: "I will sprinkle clean water on you, and you shall be clean from all your uncleannesses, and from all your idols I will cleanse you. And I will give you a new heart, and a new spirit I will put within you" (Ezek. 36:25–26).

Negotiated with a boatman to take us out on the Ganges for a few bucks. The Ganges was swirling and swollen, overflowing from the heavy monsoon rains upstream, but it was good to get away from the stench of the shore and get out on the open waters

in the gathering dusk. I wanted to see the *ghat* known as Manikarnika, the place of the burning of the dead.

Boatmen on the Ganges, Varanasi

With a little coaxing and favorable currents, the rowers got us
in for a closer look. Here fires burn continuously, consuming up
to a hundred corpses a day. Boats tethered to the shore were piled
high with the wood which fuels the eternal flame. The people
believe that to die here and to have their ashes scattered on the
Ganges leads to instant *nirvana*, freeing them from the otherwise
endless cycle of birth and rebirth. For them, this is the portal to
paradise. Immortality, though, comes with a price. The wood
has to be bought—and for the lowest caste, their dead are often
burned en masse. If they can't afford enough wood, the half-
burned corpses are simply dumped into the river. Over a century
ago, Mark Twain took a boat on the Ganges to this very point and
wrote with purposeful sarcasm of Manikarnika: "The fire used
is sacred, of course—for there is money in it. Ordinary fire is
forbidden; there is no money in it. I was told that this sacred fire

is all furnished by one person, and that he has a monopoly of it and charges a good price for it. To get to paradise from India is an expensive thing. Every detail connected with the matter costs something, and helps to fatten a priest."[13]

The bodies of men are covered in white shrouds and women in orange, and we saw two dead women being readied for the funeral pyre. Above their corpses, flames burned bright with flesh. This place has the look and smell of hell about it.

We moved on as the oarsmen pulled against the current. Last light brightened the river, but evil hung in the air along with the stench of death as night descended over the Ganges.

# 15

# The Broken Sword

**Jon Wesley and Sarah (Indonesia)**

Ye fearful saints, fresh courage take;
The clouds ye so much dread
Are big with mercy and shall break
In blessings on your head.

Judge not the Lord by feeble sense,
But trust Him for His grace.
Behind a frowning providence
He hides a smiling face.

His purposes will ripen fast,
Unfolding every hour.
The bud may have a bitter taste,
But sweet will be the flow'r.

Blind unbelief is sure to err
And scan His work in vain.
God is His own interpreter,
And He will make it plain.[1]

*William Cowper*

The first time I crossed the Atlantic was as a young sailor aboard the USS *Denebola*. The return voyage found us dodging two hurricanes. For seven days, we tacked across rolling seas. Towering waves broke over our bow as we pushed through the tempest. After scurrying along the Outer Banks to avoid yet another storm, we at last reached our safe harbor in Virginia. The captain and crew had skillfully guided the ship over thousands of miles of stormy seas and narrow channels, and at last, the port was before us. In the distance, I could see my family waiting at the dock. I was happy. I was home. It's a feeling sailors have experienced as long as people have gone to sea. Ancient mariners had a word for it—when wind and tide, rudder and sail, all worked together to bring them home or "at the port": it is *opportunity*. The word has come down from Latin, directly into our vocabulary. Mr. Webster captured that very sense of convergence in defining *opportunity* as "a combination of circumstances favorable for the purpose."[2]

The dictionary definition masks the reality that our opportunity of reaching port actually came through unfavorable circumstances: facing a storm at sea, changing course—again and again. The opportunity to go on a picnic might come through the favorable circumstances of sunny weather and a free weekend, but it's often in the storm of unfavorable circumstances that life's greatest opportunities are seen and seized. Edward Sills captured this truth vividly in his poem "Opportunity."

> This I beheld, or dreamed it in a dream:
> There spread a cloud of dust along a plain;
> And underneath the cloud, or in it, raged
> A furious battle, and men yelled, and swords
> Shocked upon swords and shields. A prince's banner
> Wavered, then staggered backward, hemmed by foes.
> A craven hung along the battle's edge,
> And thought, "Had I a sword of keener steel—
> That blue blade that the King's son bears— but this
> Blunt thing—!" He snapt and flung it from his hand,

And lowering crept away and left the field.
Then came the King's son, wounded, sore bestead,
And weaponless, and saw the broken sword,
Hilt-buried in the dry and trodden sand,
And ran and snatched it, and with battle-shout
Lifted afresh he hewed his enemy down,
And saved a great cause that heroic day.[3]

Jon Wesley and his wife Sarah have taught me so much about courage in cross-bearing, as they have followed Christ and made him known in gospel-destitute regions of Indonesia. The path to get there and stay there has been filled with pain and unanswered questions that persist to this day. Yet, they have snatched the broken sword of opportunity and embraced the suffering and joy set before them.

The two of them served Christ in China when they were first married. The happy news that they were expecting was soon shadowed by tests that revealed their baby girl would have significant physical difficulties; so they came off the field for the birth. I had returned from my first trip to Afghanistan, and Jon Wesley was at a church where I shared about the hard, life-and-death circumstances that the Christians there were joyfully pushing through for the sake of the gospel. After the service, I saw Jon Wesley, and he was literally sobbing. Without a word, I knew why. What I described of pioneer missions was what he believed God had made him and Sarah for. The compass of their lives pointed to lands and peoples who had never once heard the good news. But was that opportunity now closed to them? The prospects were bleak, considering the needs their daughter would have. He was torn by love and caught in a crossroad of question marks.

With hope in the God who gave her to them, they named their baby Zoe, meaning "life." Zoe was born with half a heart and would almost immediately require open-heart surgery to survive. In February 2009, I wrote in my journal:

This afternoon Jon Wesley called. He and Sarah have been forced to make a difficult detour on their return to serving in China. Their little four-month-old daughter underwent open-heart surgery last week. Baby Zoe is a two-foot-long fighter who came through the surgery by God's grace, and Jon Wesley called to say that Zoe was home! This is a miracle! I laughed with joy and disbelief at the sudden news. Jon Wesley and Sarah have held their little girl through the shadow of death, and in that valley they have known the fellowship of Christ's sufferings, leaving their unanswered questions at his scarred feet. Their battles between faith and doubt, joy and sorrow, life and death, perfectly speak to the truth in 2 Corinthians 4: "We are afflicted in every way, but not crushed; perplexed, but not driven to despair; persecuted, but not forsaken; struck down, but not destroyed; always carrying in the body the death of Jesus, so that the life of Jesus may also be manifested in our bodies. . . . For it is all for your sake, so that as grace extends to more and more people it may increase thanksgiving, to the glory of God. So we do not lose heart." (vv. 8–10, 15–16)

Not long afterwards, an opportunity opened for Jon Wesley and Sarah to go to Indonesia. They talked over the situation at length with Zoe's doctor. He admitted that no family in this kind of situation had ever asked him if it was OK to move to Indonesia! He reminded them that Zoe would need a second open-heart surgery around the age of three. But until then her condition could be monitored in nearby Singapore; so from a medical standpoint, he couldn't tell them not to go. And so they went. While on this short-term assignment, they learned of the gospel needs of the Riau, a people group that live on an archipelago of islands that stretch from Sumatra to the Sulu Sea. So they determined to return to Indonesia long term.

In 2012, when Zoe was three, she had her second heart surgery. Her recovery was longer than the first time, but things looked good—and the doctor again gave them a green light to go back to Indonesia. They had every reason to stay in America, but they trusted God—and therefore had every reason to go to live in Indonesia long term.

When I visited them in 2015, Zoe was six years old—and had two little brothers, Zyon and Jon Wesley Jr. And I saw that not only were Jon Wesley and Sarah making disciples on their island, but they were making forays to other islands, learning the local dialect, and "fishing for men."

## Pulau Kundur, Off the Coast of Sumatra
### *September 20, 2015*

Today we visited a family—Pak Nur and his wife, Ibu Nur—with whom Jon Wesley had had previous contact. They were happy to see him again and catch up on family news over tea and fried squid. Our conversation was interrupted by the midday call to prayer, and they excused themselves to head to the mosque. Faithful Muslims will pray five times a day, quoting these words from the Quran a total of seventeen times a day: "Show us the straight path."

After returning from Friday prayers, we sat with Pak Nur and his family. Ibu Nur shared how their daughter had given birth three weeks earlier. Ever since, she has been almost completely incapacitated and unable to care for her newborn. The local health remedies had been unsuccessful. The obvious next step was to take her to the *dukun*—the local witch doctor. Here is where the lines get fuzzy with Islam. The Riau are fiercely Muslim. However, undergirding this religious label are deep roots in animism, a belief system which holds that virtually every event in life is affected by supernatural spirits, for good or for bad. The Muslim in Pak Nur goes to the mosque to pray to Allah to secure his eternal destiny. The fisherman-animist in Pak Nur sacrifices a chicken to appease the *Hantu Laut*, the Ocean Spirit, which he believes will determine how good of a catch he'll bring in. The Riau live in constant fear—fear about whether they'll have enough to eat tomorrow and fear about what will happen when they die.

Before we left, Jon Wesley was able to plant seeds of hope. He shared from God's Word how right now Pak Nur and his family can have peace with God through Jesus Christ. He prayed for Pak Nur's daughter who was sick and asked for God to bless him with a successful day of fishing the next day, and he asked—in Jesus's name—for God to answer the prayer that he daily prays: "God, show him the straight and only path to you."

## Lengkang, Indonesia
### September 28, 2015

Went to the docks at Lengkang early this morning with Jon Wesley. Boats of all sorts bobbed about the ragged wharves where passengers waited for one of the sea taxis to their island. Jon Wesley bargained in Bahasa for our passage (thirteen dollars) to Karimun, and soon we were in open waters, sputtering past lumbering freighters plying the straits toward Singapore. Karimun is just one of a thousand inhabited islands in the archipelago, where the Riau people live. The Riau are sometimes called "sea gypsies" because their entire lives are centered on the sea.

Along the way to Karimun, Jon Wesley struck up a conversation with one of the passengers on our boat. Pak Rahmat volunteered to show us around his island, which consisted of a jigsaw of shanties on stilts, pieced together by narrow boardwalks. These places were part of the island only in a technical sense—it was like a Legoland that extended into the sea on pylons and stilts. Beneath us the water slopped with a thick coat of garbage, sewage, and whatever animal was unlucky enough to fall into the mix.

Pak Rahmat took us to the island's main attraction—the fish market, which was piled with slithering sea creatures. Jon Wesley used this as an occasion to expand his vocabulary, for a man who wants to reach fishermen better know his fish! He pointed to different ones asking, "*Apa itu?*" (What is it?) He learned that sea bass are called *lebam* and eels are *sembilang*. The women behind the table giggled at his questions but were obviously pleased that he would talk to them. One old fisherman caught on and pulled from a tub his prize catch from that morning. He held up a stingray the size of a turkey platter. The ancient mariner had a cigarette barely hanging on his lip, which bobbed with every syllable. "*Apa itu?*" Jon Wesley asked. "*Ikan pari,*" the man replied with a sprinkling of ashes. Jon Wesley went on to talk with him about fishing because he is actually fishing for this man and his people!

Jon Wesley

Afterwards we took rickshaws around the island to scout it out. Jon Wesley talked with our rickshaw driver, and though he's not yet adept in the local dialect, he could converse with this Muslim man in Bahasa. Inevitably (or I should say, intentionally) the conversation moved from pleasantries to common interests to deeper things: "What do you believe about the forgiveness of sins?"

The old man shrugged. "I do the best I can and hope Allah is kind."

"May I tell you what I believe about forgiveness?" (The Bahasa word for forgiveness is *ampun*.) And Jon Wesley told him about the *ampun* he experienced firsthand through Jesus Christ, and that through Jesus, God was both kind in forgiving sin and just in dealing with it. The Bahasa word for grace, *kasih karunia*, literally means "gift of bountiful love." God has thus shown amazing kindness to sinners like Jon Wesley and the old rickshaw driver through the most bountiful of all gifts—his Son.

Afterwards, Jon Wesley and I returned to the docks to find a boat bound for home before nightfall. As we passed the stilted shanties and market stalls crowded with people and rotting fruit, I wondered why a man would move his family halfway around the world, learn another language, take risky trips across open seas, serve in squalor and obscurity among people who are occasionally friendly, often indifferent, and sometimes quite hostile. And so I asked him why. He answered with a grin that you could see went all the way to his heart, and then he said he and Sarah "have this unshakeable feeling that God has brought us here to see what *he* is going to do, and we get to take part in it!" I think it encourages him to know that Jesus spent lots of time in boats, too, and knew everything there is to know about fishing—even where to catch them! Jon Wesley is simply pursuing the One who said to him, "Follow me, and I will make you fishers of men" (Matt. 4:19).

The sun had just sunk into the western waters when we reached Jon Wesley's place. Sarah prepared a good supper tonight, and we talked about the hundreds of islands that have yet to be reached and of the geographic, cultural, and spiritual barriers around them, which are daunting. Despite all of that, they spoke confidently of the truth that the Word of God is not bound. They are already seeing gospel light dawn in more and more hearts both in their neighborhood and on nearby islands. Even sweet little Zoe is part of this gospel force. The courage her mom and dad have been given has become hers, too. Zoe has fully embraced the life and the people here. She has a wonderful way of confidently but kindly gathering her little Muslim friends in the neighborhood and telling them about Jesus. Not long ago she took her *Jesus Storybook Bible* outside and gathered several of her friends together in a circle and was telling them Bibles stories. A couple of minutes into her "sermon," one little boy raised his hand and said, "I am a Muslim. I'm not sure I should listen to this." Zoe politely answered, "OK, you may go" and went right on telling the kids about Jesus.

True to her name, Zoe is a wonder of life and also of grace, for Jesus has carried her in his arms for more than six years now—and he always will.

Zoe with a neighbor

The following year Jon Wesley and Sarah came back to the States for the birth of their fourth child. There were some concerns about the pregnancy, and eventually tests made it clear that the boy on the way would have Down syndrome and a concomitant heart defect. The news hit hard. They had endured so much. They had come so far. Why this? Sarah was honest about her struggle beneath this crushing news. She told me she cried to the Lord: "I already have given my life to serve you in Indonesia. I already have a child with a serious heart condition. And now this? Really, God? Are you punishing us for some reason? Are you showing us we shouldn't be in Indonesia?" Sarah said she was in a wrestling match with God—and at times a one-sided shouting match—over her hard questions. Like David, who gave us language in the Psalms for our groanings of fear, pain, and confusion, she could say, "With my voice I cry out to the LORD; with my voice I plead for mercy to the LORD. I pour out my complaint before him; I tell my trouble before him. When my spirit faints within me, you know my way! . . . I cry to you, O LORD; I say, 'You are my refuge'" (Ps. 142:1–3, 5).

Baby Owen was born, and what followed was a year of surgeries and therapies and uncertainties as they prepared to return to their home in Indonesia. Despite this detour and a dark valley, God gave them light, hope, and courage to take the next step. One of those days of hope and courage came when Jon Wesley, Sarah, and Owen attended a missions conference in Minneapolis.

## Minneapolis, Minnesota
*October 15, 2016*

Today closed out our missions conference at Bethlehem Baptist Church. Having so many friends and team members here from the other side of the world has made this feel as much like a family reunion as a missions conference. Tonight we had a strong finish. John Piper preached the closing message and then—despite the late hour and a full day tomorrow of preaching—he kindly agreed to a Q&A. His answers to two of my questions were like perfectly placed arrows of wisdom and encouragement sent out to strengthen the hearts of Jon Wesley and Sarah, who were in the audience with Owen. Their anticipated departure date for returning to Indonesia is looming, but I know there are still lingering question marks.

Q&A with John Piper: "He can go. He can go."

**Keesee:** I hear couples say, "I can take that risk. I can go to the hard places." But when children come along, their God seems to get a bit smaller and they can't seem to trust him. What do you say to couples considering taking their children into harm's way?

**Piper:** Two things. First, America isn't a safe place for children, if going to hell is your biggest concern. Second thing is that I think Paul was single because of the suffering he knew he would have. When he says, "Don't I have a right to have a wife like Peter?" Peter got killed. He had a wife, and Peter was killed eventually. We don't know what happened to her. She was in danger because of Peter's life, and

Paul decided not to do that. When we look at chapter 11 of 2 Corinthians and look at what Paul endured, it seems like there wasn't a moment in his life that he could relax. There was danger everywhere. Danger from robbers. Danger on the sea. Danger on the road. Danger from brothers. Danger from Gentiles. Danger from strangers. Danger, danger, danger. I think when he pondered marriage, given that calling and what he knew it would mean, he said no. I think that may have implications for where you go if you have five kids. I don't want to be naïve and say that if a place is dangerous, it doesn't matter if you have kids. Some places a couple would be perfect. Some places a single person would be perfect. Other places a family with a bunch of kids would be perfect. Each of them dangerous, but each of them different. I don't want to say you can't put your kids in danger because clearly there are dangers everywhere. And I think historically there have been whole families who have been killed for the sake of Christ, and it has been glorious. On the other hand, I don't want to say it's a matter of indifference of where you serve. It might depend on the age of your children, the number of your children, the disability of your children. There are all kinds of factors that would cause you to say, "I don't think we are called there." But God is able to call a family with six kids to go to a place that 99 percent of the people in the world would consider a ridiculous decision.

**Keesee:** You mention families with children with disabilities. How would you advise those who want to go but face serious family challenges—children with serious medical disabilities or depression or mental disabilities?

**Piper:** You wouldn't go where it's a given that your child will die. To take a risk with your children is different than a death sentence. You weigh the kind of disability they have. There are some kinds of disabilities that are gold on the mission field and wonderfully useful. They see you loving the people they throw over the cliff or in the river. They see you raising one. What would that mean? It means you have a different God than I have. So you raise them right in front of them. But if it means you'd give your child a death sentence if you go somewhere, I doubt that you should do that. On the other hand, there are disabilities that can be hard—but it would be hard anywhere.[4]

At the end of the Q&A, Piper closed the session in prayer. At that point, he was supposed to slip out the back so he could avoid delays and get home to prepare for Sunday. Evidently, though, he didn't get the memo. Actually, what happened next reminded me that "the steps of a good man are ordered by the LORD" (Ps. 37:23 KJV). Instead of slipping behind the curtain and out the back door while closing announcements were being made, John Piper walked down the aisle to the lobby. I followed him out, and when Piper got to the lobby, he saw Jon Wesley carrying Owen, who was taken out of the session when Owen began to cry. Piper made a detour over to them, and patting Owen on the back, he said with a smile, "He can go. He can go."

———

What Jon Wesley and Sarah have learned since returning to Indonesia with their children is that rather than closing a door to ministry in Indonesia, Owen's Down syndrome has actually opened doors that they would not have otherwise had. They have seen how his disability has given them a great "back door" to Muslim families in similar situations but who are suffering in shame and silence. So a door of understanding, compassion, and therapies are opening hearts wider to the gospel that gives us all perspective and hope in our own brokenness. Sarah said, "I am learning to choose to trust God with the future instead of fearing what might happen. I choose to live life in the light of the reality of today—not in fear of what might happen in the future. If I live in fear of the what-ifs and what-might-happens of the future, I will miss the joy and opportunities God has given me today."

Owen is almost two-and-a half years old now and making good progress. He's walking and beginning to talk. Sarah said his first word was "Go!" That's a good word to begin with. It's the word that puts feet and wings and wheels to the Great Commission and that led Owen's mom and dad to the far side of the sea. And it's a good word for an energetic little boy, who I believe will go on and go far—taking up the broken sword of opportunity and, by grace, doing great things for God.

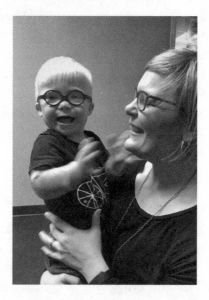

Sarah and Owen

# 16

# Aslan Is on the Move

## Micah and Katie (Oxford, England)

"In the wisdom of God, the world did not know God through wisdom." (1 Cor. 1:21)

Perhaps they make an odd pair, but the last two chapters of this book are purposely placed together. Oxford's famed colleges and churches were built centuries ago, often on foundations that go back even more centuries. All of this is well documented in history books that are themselves centuries old and housed in numerous, famous libraries throughout the city, including the Bodleian, the crown jewel of the world's libraries. In contrast, the Cambodian and Laotian villagers you will meet in the next chapter mostly live in wood and bamboo houses. As far as their "histories," these indigenous peoples didn't even have written languages until fifteen or twenty years ago—no alphabet, no books, no libraries, no schools.

Of course the contrasts between Oxford, England, and remote Ratanakiri, Cambodia, are far too numerous to list. But one example would be life expectancy. Thankfully it's edging up now, but life expectancy in that part of southeast Asia (partly because of horrific war and horrendous infant mortality rates) until recent years has been about half of what those living in England experience. When a child is sick in Oxford, the parents call a doctor; when a child is sick in Ratanakiri, the parents call a witch doctor. Despite the different remedies pursued—antibiotics versus sacrificing a water buffalo—the fear of death is shared in both places.

And though they come in different shapes and imaginations, the scholars/scientists/philologists as well as the fishermen/farmers/rubber plantation workers all worship gods of their own making. We usually imagine that a verse like "the people dwelling in darkness have seen a great light, and for those dwelling in the region and shadow of death, on them a light has dawned" (Matt. 4:16) applies to those who live in huts, wear ragged clothes, and worship things made of sticks and stones. But the truth is that the shadow falls across the entire world—even in sunlit Oxford with its soaring steeples and chic sophisticates.

While they share the darkness, it is also true that in both places "light has dawned" and continues to shine. "For as in Adam all die, so also in Christ shall all be made alive" (1 Cor. 15:22). There is only one gospel, and it is powerfully at work among preliterate animists, just as it is in one of the intellectual capitals of the world. And both witch doctors and doctors of philosophy are coming to God through Christ. There is no other way.

While on a journey to Africa, I took a detour to Oxford to catch up with two friends who have over the years seen God's grace and mercy to yet another generation in that university town.

## Port Meadow, Oxford
### *February 15, 2018*

Reached Heathrow at first light. By the time my bus made the hour-long trip from London to Oxford, the weather went from cold, misty and miserable to bright, clear, and inviting. Micah met me at the bus station, and we walked back to his place in Oxford's Jericho neighborhood, where he and his wife Katie live above her pottery shop. A strong wake-up cup served in one of Katie's creations was perfect for shaking off the short night.

My miserable night flight here brought to mind a Paul Theroux quotation: "A traveler has no power, no influence, no known identity. That is why a traveler needs optimism and heart, because without confidence, travel is misery."[1] But being with Micah has given me heart again. This brother in Christ never fails to lift my spirits nor to show what hospitality looks and feels and sounds and tastes like. Micah is a doctor of philosophy and an expert on Shakespeare, but his real gift is Barnabas-like encouragement.

After coffee and conversation, Micah and I donned our wellies and set off for Port Meadow and a tramp along the Thames. This idyllic expanse is flanked on one side by Oxford's spired cityscape and the Thames River on the other. The meadow has been kept since ancient times and is steeped in history. We are just the latest to walk these paths. I expect that long ago Roman soldiers pastured their horses here and that medieval knights jousted over these grounds. And more recently, generations of Oxford scholars have retreated here for picnics, berry-picking, and punting. I mentioned this timeline we were walking down to Micah and, as if on cue, he quoted William Blake's lines: "And did those feet in ancient time, walk upon England's mountains green: And was the holy Lamb of God, on England's pleasant pastures seen!"[2] Blake was, of course, writing poetry and not history; but these were good lines for this "pleasant pasture" as, in our turn, our boots left their mark in the mud.

We had a good long walk and talk. I'm glad to see how, even after years of living here, the pomp and circumstance of Oxford hasn't changed Micah in the ways that count. He has a love for God and a love for people that is unpretentious, because its source and force is the gospel of grace. Micah and Katie's church has given them much strength in their journey here. There they have been able to drink deeply from the Word week after week, and they've had a community in which to grow.

Micah

Not only are Micah and Katie thriving at St. Ebbe's Church, but the church is thriving, too. Actually, multiplying. Several new church plants have been started in greater Oxfordshire, and another one is underway. Micah pointed out the place along the Thames where baptisms are held. About thirty new believers were baptized here last summer. Micah said these services are celebrations of new life and are often preceded by a picnic to add even more joy to the party!

As we walked back to meet Katie, the slanting sun turned the vast, green meadow into another Narnia, as the first breath of spring was waking crocuses and snowdrops from their sleep. I thought of lines from C. S. Lewis, who also walked these very paths in his time:

Wrong will be right, when Aslan comes in sight,
At the sound of his roar, sorrows will be no more,
When he bares his teeth, winter meets its death,
And when he shakes his mane, we shall have spring again.[3]

Life is indeed stirring here—new and lasting *gospel* life—because Aslan is on the move!

## Lamb & Flag, Oxford
*February 16, 2018*

Found a corner table in an old pub once frequented by Tolkien, Lewis, and other Inklings. I'm sure I'm not the first writer who has come here hoping to get an inkling of inspiration from the location! But regardless, this is a good place to scribble a few lines and wind down the day.

I'm feeling a bit footsore. This is a walkable city, and I walked a lot of it today. The winding streets reel me in with wonder. It's a good place to wander about, get lost, and then come across a landmark that seems familiar only because it's always been in my imagination. This place is magical.

I've been to so many quads, chapels, and churches that I've lost track of all the names, but Micah knows the thirty-some colleges that collectively make up the University of Oxford like the back of his hand and has access to many places that are generally off-limits, except to card-carrying scholars. To help me get oriented, Micah took me to St. Mary's, an ancient church on High Street, and we climbed its thirteenth-century tower for the best view of Oxford. From its wind-swept battlement, we had a grand view of this grand old city. The Radcliffe Camera looked like a jewel set in a green square surrounded by a tightly knit neighborhood of gold-and-gargoyle-appointed colleges.

From various gates up and down High Street, LGBT flags snapped in the breeze. This is Pride Month, and no independently minded institution of higher learning would dream of being left out. In this case, Pride—like all pride—is just another name for defiance of God. It's interesting, however, that despite the strong and fashionable secularism that dominates the colleges, there is "presence in the absence," as one Christian academic I talked with put it.

Oxford is deeply and historically rooted in the Christian faith, and the architecture, ornamentation, and even the school calendar all clearly reflect Christianity. The "stones speak," as it were. Even Oxford's motto, *Dominus Illuminatio Mea*, which is carved in stone, gilded in heraldic form, and printed in books, points to God. It is the opening line of Psalm 27: "The LORD is my light." And by grace, walking the streets and in the classrooms and quads are living epistles, like Micah—redeemed ones who can with confidence in Christ complete the verse: "The LORD is my light and my salvation; whom shall I fear? The LORD is the stronghold of my life; of whom shall I be afraid?" (Ps. 27:1).

We came down from this amazing perch, explored a bit more, and then had a proper tea—which always means good cream tea, served in silver, with perfect scones topped with a dollop of clotted cream and lashed with jam. Yes. That's a proper tea!

We returned home before Katie's shop closed because I wanted to see her in action. The big shop window of Illyria Pottery was tastefully appointed with her latest creations, and her cat, Lucie Maud, was keeping vigil. Lucie Maud is a bit of a neighborhood sensation, and passersby know she will be looking out on the street with a cultivated mixture of curiosity and indifference.

Katie was at the wheel forming a vase. Spring is in the wings, and her Oxford neighbors will want to bring some of its flowering beauty inside their homes; so Katie will be ready. It was amazing to see all that her hands have made—the pieces on the shop shelves, those waiting for the kiln, and the ones taking shape in her skillful grasp. Katie's creativity combines motion and precision, turning clay into beautiful, useful objects.

Katie at the wheel
Photo by Dean Hearne

After she closed up shop, we all went upstairs for supper and a quiet evening. I love to see how the two of them, despite their busy, demanding lives in the business and academic worlds of Oxford, really keep God in the center of it all. It's evident in their conversations, plans, and hospitality, which is a hallmark of their marriage.

## From Addison's Walk, Oxford
### *February 17, 2018*

This morning Micah and I took another long walk. Our trek eventually brought us to Addison's Walk. Beneath a brilliant sky, swans slid along the banks of the Cherwell. Snowdrops and daffodils dappled the river's edge. A heron, frightened up by a kayaker, suddenly swept across our way. With strong wings, he snapped gravity's hold, pulling along his spindly legs as an afterthought.

This picturesque path is famed for the late-night conversation almost ninety years ago that J. R. R. Tolkien and Hugo Dyson had with their atheist friend C. S. Lewis. That walk and talk would be a turning point to God for Lewis. I think what Lewis said in *Surprised by Joy* about certain books could also be said for the company he kept that night: "A young man who wishes to remain a sound Atheist cannot be too careful of his reading. There are traps everywhere. . . . God is, if I may say it, very unscrupulous."[4]

Shaken out of his purely material world of atheism, Lewis discovered that the inconsolable longings he had experienced throughout his life—what he called "stabs of joy"—were signposts to God. After his conversion he could say, "If I find in myself a desire which no experience in this world can satisfy, the most probable explanation is that I was made for another world."[5] With new eyes he saw and wrote of the beauty, glory, and joy set before him in Christ. And he brought millions along with him to see beyond what we can see—to get a glimpse of Aslan's country.

I love the lines in Lewis's sermon, "The Weight of Glory," that he preached at St. Mary's church just a short walk from here. This captures how radically transformed his outlook was since becoming a Christian: "If we consider the unblushing promises of reward and the staggering nature of the rewards promised in the Gospels, it would seem that Our Lord finds our desires not too strong, but too weak. We are half-hearted creatures, fooling about with drink and sex and ambition when infinite joy is offered us, like an ignorant child who wants to go on making mud pies in a slum because he cannot imagine what is meant by the offer of a holiday at the sea. *We are far too easily pleased.*"[6]

I asked Micah what pressures he and other Christians face at Oxford. While bigotry toward evangelicals is common across the academic world, Micah said in his experience he has only met with respectful questions. "I think perhaps the darkness is most sensed in the false assumption that *thinking people* cannot submit to the God of the Scriptures and that the light of Christian truth is in some ways of thought seemingly incongruous with the 'life of the mind.' But that is a false contrast. The Academy is not the enemy, and it is not devoid of Christians. There are several Christian academics throughout Oxford, many in leading roles within the University. The light still shines in the darkness!"

We found a bench along the path, and Micah continued: "The attitude I usually encounter is that religion in any form may be fine for some as a pleasant tradition, but to live a life remolded by the gospel and that bows to God's commands is outmoded at best and potentially harmful at worst. The exclusivity of Christ and his claims as the Way, the Truth, and the Life are the most threatening ideas to a pluralistic ideal. The gospel's message is countercultural in our current context because Christ, as Sovereign, cannot share power."

However, Micah was honest to say that actually the greatest pressures are from within. That surprised me. Not because it's not true but because it is *so* true—so true for me, too. He's focused on his own walk with God both in his personal life and in his marriage. The academic world is filled with a desire to be remembered, to leave a mark, to climb to the top, to shove to the front. And so, there's a struggle with the pride of life and all the ways pride works its way out of the heart and mind. I was deeply touched and convicted by his words. Micah said the gospel's power to transform his life and his marriage has actually been the starting point of many gospel conversations for both him and Katie. They truly live the motto "The Lord Is My Light." And through their light and that of other believers here, it can be said, "The light shines in the darkness, and the darkness has not overcome it" (John 1:5).

## Oxford, England

### *Sunday, February 18, 2018*

Set out this morning with Micah and Katie for St. Ebbe's. Their church is usually only a fifteen-minute walk away, but I slowed them down by reading plaques and taking pictures, because around every corner is a reminder in stone of the centuries of God's grace and gospel at work here. John Wycliffe and William Tyndale, the two men most responsible for giving us an English Bible, walked these same streets in their time. As we walked up Broad Street, a cross in the middle of the road marked the spot where Latimer, Ridley, and Cranmer were burned at the stake during the Reformation. We hurried on past John Wesley's meeting place and reminders of England's Great Awakening in the eighteenth century. For me it was a walking church history tour. For Micah and Katie, it was a walk in the neighborhood. Despite my being a drag, we reached St. Ebbe's on time.

I've heard so much about the impact of this church, so it's good to finally be here. I recall a passage in Carolyn Weber's book where a church member said, "I chose St. Ebbe's as my home church because the gospel was taught with all due respect and care, and yet it was apparent that the congregation was having fun. . . . To put it simply, I guess, it's because I found that the people here, for the most part, take the gospel seriously without taking themselves too seriously."[7]

I noticed a good mix of generations in the service, and I know from Micah that there's a good mix of people, too—teachers and students, families and singles, the well-off and the homeless. The church gives special attention to the poor in this parish but also has a vibrant college ministry throughout Oxford. This morning's service had about three hundred, and this was the first of four services held here each Sunday in order to accommodate everyone.

Clearly, this is a praying church—something I had already heard from a missionary friend who was a member here before going to Iraq. His journey into pioneer missions began years ago at a prayer meeting here at St. Ebbe's, and today the worship leader invited any interested to gather for prayer after the service on behalf of the plans for another church plant in the area.

Walking to church: The cross in the street marks the site where the Oxford Martyrs were burned at the stake.

Pastor Vaughan Roberts was continuing his series in Galatians, and today he preached from chapter 5. Vaughan was both personable and focused as he walked us through the text. He summarized this portion of Galatians by reminding us of several things: First, don't make a religion out of rules. Second, don't make a religion out of personal freedom. Third, the boundaries and balance of this freedom are centered in the cross. In fact, there is a boundlessness of depth and height found in the freedom that Christ alone gives.[8]

The music was vibrant, and we closed by joining with joyful voices in celebration of such grace.

> There is no deeper peace than this,
> No other kindness can compare:
> He clothes us in his righteousness,
> Forever free, forever heirs.
>
> There is no sound that's like the song
> That rises up from grateful saints:
> We once were lost but now we're found;
> One with him, we bear his name.
>
> Oh praise the only One
> Who shines brighter than ten thousand suns.
> Death and hell call him victorious,
> Praise Him![9]

After church, Katie, Micah, and I went back out to Port Meadow. In good English fashion, the weather had changed from spring-like to winter-lite. Across the meadow, the few horses left to graze stood stiff. Only their manes moved in the brisk breeze that carried scattered snowflakes with it. Looking back toward the city, the spires seemed to have shrunk beneath the weight of the low, gray sky, and the meadow had lost much of the showy colors we walked through the other day. But though the sky is heavy, my heart is light. The lines we just sang this morning continue to rise:

> There is no sound that's like the song
> That rises up from grateful saints.[10]

Saints past, present, and those yet to come are all bound together by grace and gratitude. Jesus is doing something in this

center of learning that is truly brilliant, and he is building something in this ancient place that is truly lasting—saving all who
come to him. Christ's unending life guarantees it, and his grace
means glory far beyond anything that can be seen in this faint
light. Like Lewis, I also feel a stab of joy over what's to come.

# 17

# End of the Road

## JD Crowley (Cambodia, Laos)

"The kingdoms and governments of this world have frontiers
that must not be crossed. The gospel of Jesus Christ knows no
frontier. It never has been kept within bounds."[1]

*Samuel Zwemer*

Alan Seeger, a war poet who fought and died in the Great War,
left us these haunting lines:

I have a rendezvous with Death
At some disputed barricade
Where Spring comes round with rustling shade
And apple blossoms fill the air.
I have a rendezvous with Death
When Spring brings back blue days and fair. . . .

But I've a rendezvous with Death
At midnight in some flaming town,

When Spring trips north again this year,
And I to my pledged word am true,
I shall not fail that rendezvous.[2]

Seeger was true to his word. He was cut down in a coura-geous, but costly, charge across no-man's-land in the Battle of the Somme in 1916. He was twenty-eight years old. The power of Seeger's poem is not just its prescience; it's an elegy for every-one—in war and in peace—because death reigns worldwide. But in some places and times it *rages*, as it did in Seeger's day. History is filled with such times and places that are stained with blood, scarred with mass graves, and where death is a way of life.

Cambodia is such a place.

Forty years ago, during the time of Communist leader Pol Pot, one out of five Cambodians died at the hands of their own coun-trymen—starved to death, worked to death, or just murdered en masse.[3] As historian Philip Short put it, "It was not simply that life had no value; that killing became an act of no consequence. . . . The holocaust that consumed Cambodia required the com-plicity of so large a proportion of the population that one has to ask how the victims would have behaved if the roles had been reversed."[4]

Now imagine going to the weakest and poorest peoples of Cambodia, marginalized tribes living on the edge of the coun-try both geographically and socially, a people whose language had never been written (why bother?). The tribes have long been only a source of slaves for more powerful people, and slaves don't need to read or write. From the time they come into their dis-mal world, they are taught that their hardships, their sicknesses, even the shadow of death that darkens their days are all because the spirits of their ancestors curse them from the grave. One day, when they too slip into the final night, they will doubtless curse their children, too. They can give as good as they get. And there are darker, more powerful spirits who control the outcome of their days—demon spirits, unseen, yet everywhere, who add to their weight of misery. These dark spirits require money to the witch doctor and animal sacrifices in order to be temporarily satisfied. The people have been cheated so often at this game that the rules have become their religion.

This unwaking nightmare was the reality for these unreached tribes—until gospel light broke the night! As Isaiah, looking toward Christ, said, "The people who walked in darkness have seen a great light; those who dwelt in a land of deep darkness, on them has light shown. You have multiplied the nation; you have increased its joy; they rejoice before you as with joy at the harvest" (Isa. 9:2–3). This passage is a beautiful portrait of what happened in the remote province of Ratanakiri, Cambodia. Beginning in the 1990s, in the span of a single generation, my friends JD and Kim Crowley and their children, along with several other intrepid families, planted themselves among the unreached Tampuan, Krung, and Jarai people. They put their languages into written form and gave them their first book—the Book of books. New life stirred, and vibrant churches formed among these people. When I first visited, these missionaries were blazing trails both linguistically and literally as they traveled as far as the road would take them—and then walked on in order to spread the fame of Jesus to every corner of this remote borderland.

Years later, I returned to Ratanakiri to visit JD and the rest of this company of heroes. What I found could well be described as a missions miracle. In the missions world, it is common to speak of "planting self-sustaining churches," "churches that will plant churches, that will plant churches, that will plant churches," and "training national leaders." But in far too many cases none of this ever really happens. The "national leaders" are more like local employees, and churches whose growth has been built on the shifting sand of missionary money are shaky, leaning westward, and too feeble to reproduce on their own. But what I found in Ratanakiri was remarkable. The every-tribe-every-tongue gospel was at work in every tongue (and script) of every tribe in the region, and it was now the Krung, Tampuan, and Jarai that were taking the lead in reaching and teaching their people.

It's easy to summarize such results in a few lines, but this truncates the years and tidies up the frayed edges of pain and loss. Cross-bearing always involves cost, especially when undertaking a direct and relentless assault on the gates of hell. John Piper defined such gospel advance as "back-breaking, culture-penetrating, darkness-shattering initial work."[5] The pain and joy of cross-bearing by pioneer missionaries and linguists have given entrance to this death-defying gospel in a place where only death has reigned. Christ, by his cross and resurrection, is giving life to "all those who through fear of death were subject to lifelong slavery" (Heb. 2:15). Jesus has, as songwriter Andrew Peterson put it, "beaten death at death's own game."[6]

## Phnom Penh, Cambodia
### *August 2, 2015*

Arrived in Phnom Penh late last night after a bouncing descent through tumultuous monsoon skies—it was a like a carnival ride through the stratosphere! The airport was newer and shinier than the one I landed at here sixteen years ago, but passports and visas, it seemed, were handled by the same sluggish, rubberstamp-wielding bureaucrats as back then. They made me wish I was back upstairs dodging thunderbolts. I eventually escaped the stranglehold and found JD patiently waiting, reading, and nursing a cappuccino at Costa Coffee outside the arrivals hall.

It's good to be back with my friend in his country and among his people. JD is a pioneer missionary and linguist who can say with the apostle Paul, "It has always been my ambition to preach the gospel where Christ was not known" (Rom. 15:20 NIV). He and his family are part of a remarkable team of missionaries and Bible translators who have done just that among the hill tribes along Cambodia's northern frontier and in the borderlands of Vietnam and Laos.

JD Crowley

Set out this morning to explore the capital. It's the middle of the rainy season here, and the streets were filled with mud from last night's downpour. The heart of the old city sits at the confluence of two great rivers: the Mekong and the Tonle Sap. The banks were brimming with roiling, mocha-colored waters. The king's palace and royal pagoda sit across a broad promenade near this rendezvous of the rivers. Like the gilded paint that highlights the royal residence, the Cambodian king's power is mostly show. The real power is held by Hun Sen, a former Khmer Rouge commander who turned from Communism to the kind of strong-man democracy common in Southeast Asia. His long tenure as prime minister is a shadow that leads back to the darkest time in Cambodia's history: the years of Pol Pot.

The Khmer Rouge (that is, the "Red" or Communist forces) were the hideous offspring of the North Vietnamese Communists. The

Khmer Rouge festered on the fringes of the country, gradually taking more and more territory and completing their stranglehold by taking Phnom Penh in 1975. Like all Communists coming to power, Pol Pot, the Khmer Rouge's leader, promised Cambodians a whole new world. Instead what they got was a quick trip to hell. Pol Pot's rule lasted for four long, miserable years, during which time his only talent as a leader seemed to be mass murder. Nearly two million Cambodians—or one out of every five—died during Pol Pot's reign of terror.

I asked JD to take me out to Choueng Ek, often simply called the Killing Fields. There were thousands of killing fields across the country, but this one was preserved and an ossuary built to house the remains of some of the twenty thousand killed here by the Khmer Rouge. Inside the memorial, skulls were stacked to the sky, and murder weapons were on display along the base, ones that underscored how crude and brutal the killing here was—bullets, clubs, bamboo sticks, a hoe, an ax. The scale of this was shocking, but the grounds outside the ossuary were sickening. Dozens of depressions in the ground marked the sites of mass graves, and a great tree still stands—a place where infants were killed by smashing them against the trunk. Being there was like walking through a crime scene, literally, as the rain continues to bring up victims' clothes, blindfolds, even their bones.

This afternoon, I went to Tuol Sleng, the Auschwitz of Cambodia. I walked through this former high school, where over the space of three years as many as twenty thousand were held and tortured to death. What was especially grievous and insane about the murders at Tuol Sleng was the careful and creative attention given to torture. Death could have been quick—a bullet to the head or, to save precious ammunition, a hoe whack to the skull. But death was not the objective so much as suffering, and to intensify suffering, prisoners were not allowed to cry out—else they were given shocks with an electric wire. They would weep but not scream, suffering to death in silence.

Pol Pot's torturers were careful to photograph all their victims—before and sometimes after being tortured. Many of these photographs were glued to the walls, where once chalkboards hung and students' chatter sounded. The yellowing pictures show mostly youthful prisoners, young men and women, even children. Their expressions vary. For some, their eyes show fear, others defiance, and some show peace. Many Christians were martyred during Pol Pot's bloody rule. Among the hundreds of fading photographs are, no doubt, the faces of my brothers and sisters.

Tuol Sleng: "I wish I knew her name."

The afternoon sun slanted through the windows, casting the shadows of the prison bars that remain here across the faces of the victims. And for a moment, it seemed that the ghosts of Tuol Sleng stirred, for the photographs haunt me. One in particular I can't get away from. A young woman wears a prison uniform tagged with the number twenty-one hanging from a safety pin. The soiled shirt is likely a hand-me-down pulled off an earlier victim. The right shoulder is torn. The buttons appear hastily—no doubt nervously—buttoned. She has been struck in the mouth, but the wound is starting to heal. She looks straight into the camera, straight into the face of her killer. Her wide, dark eyes hold her last words. They speak of dignity and courage and sorrow over such an end. I wish I knew her name.

### Ban Lung, Ratanakiri, Cambodia
*August 4, 2015*

Got to JD's after nightfall. The clank of cowbells and chorus of night creatures mingled with a Buddhist funeral chant makes for an odd lullaby, as the sun pulls a starry blanket over Ratanakiri. This is Cambodia's northeast province, bordering on Vietnam and Laos. During the Vietnam War, the Ho Chi Minh Trail snaked through here, and massive bomb craters from the B-52s still pocket the land. It's a remote frontier country, home to a mosaic of tribes, such as the Tampuan, Krung, Brao, and Jarai. Twenty-five years ago there wasn't a single Christian among these groups, nor did most of them even have a written language. Now there are vibrant congregations among all of these tribes, and the Bible is read and preached and shared in their languages! "This is the LORD's doing; it is marvelous in our eyes" (Ps. 118:23).

It was so good to see Kim and their son Nathaniel again. This will be my home away from home for the next few days. In preparing my room, Kim found an enormous scorpion who evidently was planning his own welcome. She put him in a jar to show me—it was the biggest scorpion I've ever seen. I'll tuck in the mosquito netting a little tighter tonight!

## Krala Village, Ratanakiri
*August 5, 2015*

Christians of the Krung and Brao tribes have organized their own Bible school, which gathers twice a year in various villages, this time in Krala. The leader of the school is a Krung pastor named Naay. He was one of the early believers among the Krung. That was almost twenty years ago, and since that time he has become not only a faithful pastor but also a Bible teacher and a mentor of men. In recent years, since the creation of a Krung alphabet, he has assisted with Bible translation work and promoted literacy among his people. Naay is a five-talent servant, always laboring to increase the fame of his Master.

The first Bible school was started by JD and the other missionaries here. It was taught in the national language of Khmer so that different tribal groups could participate. Students were charged to attend the school, and tuition was a sack of rice—their food share. They also had to find their own way to get there—usually by foot or by bicycle. Some Jarai Christians in outlying areas made a sixteen-hour journey by bike—each carrying their sack of rice. Some criticized this approach saying it was wrong to treat poor people this way, but JD and the others started out by planting well—not by sprinkling the "Miracle-Gro" of money but by preparing good soil and letting the seed of the Word do its work. This made the Christians here strong to take root, grow, and branch out. Consequently, after a few years the different tribes were able to start their own "mother tongue" Bible schools. As JD and his colleagues told them, "This will be your school, your language, your teachers, your money."

Today Naay taught from Matthew 20:1–16:

> For the kingdom of heaven is like a master of a house who went out early in the morning to hire laborers for his vineyard. After agreeing with the laborers for a denarius a day, he

sent them into his vineyard. And going out about the third hour he saw others standing idle in the marketplace, and to them he said, "You go into the vineyard too, and whatever is right I will give you." So they went. Going out again about the sixth hour and the ninth hour, he did the same. And about the eleventh hour he went out and found others standing. And he said to them, "Why do you stand here idle all day?" They said to him, "Because no one has hired us." He said to them, "You go into the vineyard too." And when evening came, the owner of the vineyard said to his foreman, "Call the laborers and pay them their wages, beginning with the last, up to the first." And when those hired about the eleventh hour came, each of them received a denarius. Now when those hired first came, they thought they would receive more, but each of them also received a denarius. And on receiving it they grumbled at the master of the house, saying, "These last worked only one hour, and you have made them equal to us who have borne the burden of the day and the scorching heat." But he replied to one of them, "Friend, I am doing you no wrong. Did you not agree with me for a denarius? Take what belongs to you and go. I choose to give to this last worker as I give to you. Am I not allowed to do what I choose with what belongs to me? Or do you begrudge my generosity?" So the last will be first, and the first last.

Naay did not call this parable by its usual name—"The Parable of the Workers in the Vineyard." Rather he called it "The Parable of the Merciful Boss." Naay pointed out that most of us are not comfortable with this story. We look at ourselves as those who worked hard all day and the master as unfair, but that's because we think too much of ourselves and too little of the Master. We are all eleventh-hour people—those who have been shown unearned, unexpected generosity!

As Naay was laying out these truths from the passage, I could hear JD whispering in the conversational prayer that is his habit,

"He's preaching grace now. Lord, help them to get this. Give them understanding."

The Lord did indeed answer JD's prayer, for I received fresh insight into this parable—a needed rebuke and overwhelming joy in the lavish grace of my merciful Boss.

## Kachong Village, Ratanakiri Near the Vietnamese Border
*August 7, 2015*

JD had to deliver a door to a church among the Tampuan people. They had built the place themselves but did not have a door for the building. He joked that it was called "The Church of the Open Door." He had a door to deliver, but I had another mission for our trip today. Sixteen years ago when I was last in Ratanakiri, JD and I took a young mother who was sick with malaria to a hospital here. The woman's daughter, named Chee, was about nine years old at the time. She stayed and took care of her mom night and day. I took a picture of Chee standing in the door of her mom's room at the hospital. The floor was covered with urine, blood, and flies, but there Chee was—a little girl doing a woman's work. Whatever happened to Chee? What does she look like now? Does she have a family of her own? I wanted to find out for myself. I framed a copy of the picture to give to her as a gift if I could find her.

Over the years, JD had lost track of the little girl, but through a friend of a friend he found out that Chee is married (I guess she would be about twenty-five years old now) and the name of her village. The road we took was one I remembered from years past, only then it was a mud strip that ended in a dense jungle. What I saw was shocking. The great green forest with trees a dozen feet in diameter was all gone. They paved paradise and put up a rubber plantation. For miles in all directions, the forest is gone, replaced by orderly rows of rubber saplings. Hundreds of thousands of acres in Cambodia, especially in tribal areas, have been taken and given as concessions to Vietnamese and Chinese business interests. This is what a land grab looks like.

Drove on toward the Vietnamese border to Kachong, Chee's village, in hopes of finding her. There are no addresses, though. Cambodians have an expression, "the mouth is the road"—that is, go as far as you can, then ask. You might then get one step closer—a bit like a game of Clue. Eventually, with the help of several "mouths," we were directed to a particular hut in the jumble of Chee's village. And there she was—the mother of two now, cradling a nursing newborn. She remembered JD and had fond memories of his children, her old playmates. She was surprised and delighted to see the picture I brought. We stayed only briefly but promised to return when Chee's husband was home. Plus, JD had a plan. In the village where we were delivering the church door is a young woman named Yett, who, like Chee, is of the Tampuan tribe. Yett is famous for evangelism—a wise and committed disciple-maker. So JD wanted to connect Yett with Chee to share the gospel and study the Word together.

Yett: the Wesley and Watts of the Tampuan people

JD introduced me to Yett and her family. Yett's life is a beautiful love story, for she was a poor, illiterate, tribal girl—all the descriptors of someone who is mostly accounted as worthless here. But when Jesus set his everlasting love on her, everything changed! Yett came from a long line of demon-worshipers, but as a girl she longed to know who created all that she saw. Her grandmother said that she had heard his name was Bakatoy—"the God of the Skies"—but no one among their people knew him. Then Yett's father became a Christian after he heard the gospel from believers among the Jarai tribe, whose language he could understand. Through these Jarai evangelists, Yett heard the gospel and believed on the Lord Jesus, knowing at once that this was "the God of the Skies," her Creator and now Redeemer, the only true God. Though she never went to school, the Lord gave her the ability to read and write in three languages, and he put new songs in her heart. In fact, she wrote and compiled the first hymnal for her people—Yett is the Wesley and Watts of the Tampuan people! I asked her if she would sing one for me before we headed over to Chee's village. And so she and her brother sang the gospel:

> In the past we didn't know God the Father.
> Yes, in the past we didn't know Bakatoy.
> God is the One who sent Jesus Christ.
> This Jesus is the Lord who came down to save us.
> Come, bow down before the Lord Jesus, who forgives sin.
> Come, all peoples of the earth,
> Hurry and believe on the Lord Jesus.

Returned to Chee's village at last light, met her husband, and introduced Yett and Chee to each other. Chee happily agreed to Yett's request to come back and study the Bible together. It brought me much joy to think that a picture taken of a little girl years ago was a sovereign snapshot—one that would be added to the album of kingdom advance as the gospel goes to another remote corner of Cambodia.

## Krala Village, Ratanakiri
*August 8, 2015*

This morning I returned to the Bible school for the closing day of teaching and worship. When we arrived, we were greeted by the sound of singing and dancing and the playing of gongs. If I could summarize the song they played, it would be, "Because of Jesus, let the nations be glad!" From the beginning, the missionaries encouraged the believers to use their traditional musical forms in worship, which included their most important instrument: the gong. But their conscience wouldn't allow this because of the association of the gong with demon worship. The missionaries pulled back but reminded them that Satan was a usurper and a thief and that the gong belonged to God. "One day," they said, "you will worship God with the gong." Eventually, Naay came to the missionaries and said, "It's time. We are ready." Naay brought together old and young to explain the decision and spent a day using the gongs in musical worship of the true and living God. JD said, "That was a glorious day!"

Naay is now training the younger generation to use the gongs and other instruments. One village elder told Naay, "All of us have sold our gongs to buy cell phones and boom boxes, and now it's only Christians who are teaching the next generation to play these instruments."

They invited me to join in their joy, assigning me the simplest of their gongs to play—what JD calls "the dummy gong." Their five-note system sounds thin and high, like bamboo; and with an old flip-flop as my drumstick, I marked the beat. But evidently I've got no rhythm, because Naay said to JD, "*Aut kaat tay,*" which means, "This isn't working." And they took my gong away. But the praise continued as the gong players and dancers circled and sang. The sound was Krung, but the taste was heaven.

## Yak Lom, Ratanakiri
### *Evening, August 8, 2015*

The day is drawing down. After the Krung Bible School finished, JD and I grabbed an early supper and then headed to Yak Lom. Like a jewel set in the jungle, Yak Lom is a perfectly round crater lake in the cavity of an ancient volcano. It's become something of a tourist attraction since I swam here years ago, and a large dock has been built at one end; but thankfully it's mostly deserted tonight.

When we drove into Yak Lom, there was a ticket booth at the entrance (another addition since I was last here). JD chatted away in Tampuan with several men hanging out at the booth. As we left them and drove on to the lake, I mentioned to JD that he had forgotten to buy our admission tickets. He replied matter-of-factly, "I created their alphabet—they don't charge me." I had a good laugh over the "price of admission" and the pretty exclusive exception clause they have at the ticket booth!

The westering sun is turning the lake into a magic mirror, perfectly reflecting the face of the sky and the waves, catching the colors of gold and vermillion. It looks like a Monet canvas.

It's good to hit the brakes and talk. We joked about the free admission and, more importantly, talked about all that has followed from the gift of written language for the tribal people here. JD gave this gift to the Tampuan people. Others of his coworkers here gave written language to the Krung and the Jarai—first an alphabet and then the Bible, which fueled every dimension of the church here: its depth and growth and reach. It's also driven the rise of literacy, as students quickly became teachers.

JD brought up a recent book by the skeptic Bart Ehrman, who said that Peter's epistles could not possibly be written by the illiterate Galilean fisherman.[7] Ehrman's provocative prose might sell well in the West, but his lazy research would be exposed here by men and women who know better. JD said that there are about two thousand tribal people who can now read after having a script for just fifteen years—and this has happened without a penny of government or NGO support. They taught each other, motivated by a desire to read the Bible! And the Khmer alphabet that is used in the tribal scripts is famous for being one of the hardest alphabets in the world to learn. Many of these two thousand have learned to read in three different languages during that fifteen-year period. Among Christians the literacy rate is well over 50 percent and is spread across all demographics—men and women, children and elderly. In every group the literacy rate has skyrocketed, even in villages where there is no formal education, such as Sakrieng, where Yett lives. There has never been a school in Sakrieng, and still the literacy rate is around 80 percent—all because of Christianity.

So if it takes just fifteen years for two thousand tribal people who belong to a culture with zero history of literacy to learn to read and write, even to the point of being able to put together hymnbooks and translate Scripture, why would it be impossible for Peter to be able to read and write? He came from a culture that had a history of literacy that stretched back more than a thousand years, a culture that prized writing and even had synagogue literacy programs. JD joked, "Poor Peter should have been born an illiterate, tribal person. Then he would have had a chance to write 1 and 2 Peter!" We both agreed that Bart needs to get out of his office and see how the real world works.

Deep dusk is settling over Yak Lom, and the dark forest is stirring with night creatures tuning up for their evening concert. It's our signal to head home.

### Pakxé, Laos
*August 12, 2015*

JD and I set out at first light on a scouting trip into Laos. It took much of a day's journey over bad roads to get to the Bolaven Plateau. A patchwork of people groups live here, including the Brao, who are ethnic and linguistic cousins to our brother Naay's tribe, the Krung. The gospel has come to the Krung and Brao of Cambodia, but the Brao of Laos are unreached and—to us—largely unlocated. Over the next few days, we hope to begin to fill in that map.

For JD, this is the next frontier for gospel advance. Laos is a hard place. Its Communist government has been brutal toward the tiny networks of evangelical house churches in the cities. In the tribal areas, such as we are in now, the authorities fear any-thing that smacks of secession. Even material in tribal languages is opposed because it empowers their identity. Ethnic Lao people are a little more than 50 percent of the population of Laos and assert their control over every corner of the country and over all the minority tribes. However, this poor, landlocked country is opening up to tourists and their much needed dollars, so into this breach we will enter. Our plan is to look like good, dumb tourists carrying clunky cameras around our neck and seeing the sites along the picturesque Bolaven Plateau. Then as we backtrack, hopefully we will find Brao people along the way, give them gos-pel material in their language, and then head for the border. If we stay out of trouble, more targeted outreach can follow, especially by the Krung churches in Cambodia.

After reaching Pakxé, the gateway to the Bolaven Plateau, we stowed our stuff, downed some stout Laotian coffee, and set out for Tad Fane. In a constellation of waterfalls in this region, Tad Fane is the North Star. It's easy to act like gawking tourists here because this ribbon of singing silver cutting through emer-ald green hills is absolutely stunning. A path led to the base of the falls through great Sarlao trees perhaps twenty feet in cir-cumference. The sound was as amazing as the sight. A rickety, rotting observation deck led to a little prominence in the river, each place more splendid than before. The force of the falls was so great that the mist swirled like cold steam. Rain and spray and mist made the place a giant jacuzzi! We heard the voice of many waters and washed in the wonder of it. There we worshiped the One who made all these things. As David said in the Psalms, "There is none like you among the gods, O Lord, nor are there any works like yours. All the nations you have made shall come and worship before you, O Lord, and shall glorify your name. For you are great and do wondrous things" (Ps. 86:8–10). "All the na-tions" include the tribes of southern Laos, and so we prayed that

God would be our Shepherd and Shield as we seek out the people he is preparing to hear his Word.

## South of Attapeu, Laos
### *August 14, 2015*

This morning we set out early, crossing the Xe Kong and driving into a town where we hoped to start our search for Brao people. Starting at the market, we played the parts of picture-taking tourists: buying baskets, admiring tubs of catfish, and quietly feeling sorry for the tree lizards awaiting someone's kettle. While we looked things over and prayed in our hearts, we met a woman selling vegetables and doughnuts with her daughters. JD tried out some Krung words to see if she understood—and she did! She was Brao—our first connection! So if a Brao woman is selling in the market, there must be a Brao village nearby. But where?

In order to lower suspicion by going to the officials instead of sneaking around them and hoping to find an English speaker (since we couldn't speak Lao or Brao), we went to a government office to ask if there was a tribal village nearby. By God's grace, two officials at city hall spoke good English and gave us directions to a nearby Brao village. Wow! Did Jesus not say, "Ask, and it will be given to you; seek, and you will find" (Matt. 7:7)?

JD drove on, looking for telltale signs like the shape and pattern of the backpack baskets, which are the fingerprints of different tribes here. Along the road, we spotted a Brao-looking house with split bamboo walls, which looked like a big basket on stilts. It drew us in. In the back, a blacksmith was busy over hot coals, forging scrap metal into machetes and knives. With a few questions, JD knew they were Brao people! The smith's name is Mang, and his wife Kon sat nearby with their son. Several neighbors quickly gathered, and JD gave them a copy of a "Creation to Christ" video—the first film ever produced in their tribal language. Within a minute, they and the DVD had disappeared into a nearby hut—and soon the creation story could be heard wafting out a window. The "old, old story" is quite new here!

As we drove on and plotted our next move, suddenly we were stopped at a makeshift checkpoint, and a man with an ancient Kalashnikov wanted to know what we were doing. This unexpected encounter led to an invitation to the village meetinghouse nearby, where we met the village chief and the head of the local militia. We were well-received, and JD gave them copies of the Creation to Christ video as gifts of thanks for their hospitality. This surprising interruption began with a gun and ended with the gospel! I thought of the passage where Paul said, "The word of God is not bound!" (2 Tim. 2:9).

Set out for the border in case the police were alerted to our activity in the tribal areas. We wanted to cross into Cambodia before nightfall, so we had a long drive ahead of us. We were making good time until a rear tire blew to shreds. I was thankful it wasn't a front tire that blew, which would have been disastrous. But JD went to work like a pit crew chief, pulling out a spare that to me looked only slightly better than the one we were replacing. In short order, we were on our way.

Three hours later we cleared the last police checkpoint and crossed into Cambodia with much joy. We now have hard facts— at least a few more—to inform our prayers and plans for further gospel advance in Laos. Isaiah's words came alive today where my King said, "I am the LORD your God who takes hold of your right hand and says to you, Do not fear; I will help you" (Isa. 41:13 NIV).

## Som Rah Village, Ratanakiri
### *Sunday, August 16, 2015*
Set out early for the Krung village of Som Rah, where Naay, who led the Krung Bible School, pastors. I wanted to see this dear brother once more before I head home. Naay's village is one of the most remote because tribal people keep getting shoved

further and further to the edges of the region. They are being pushed out to make room for vast rubber plantations that can cover thousands of acres. The one we drove through today looked like a million trees, each identically lanced to bleed white sap, which pools in collection cups. Once the rapidly growing trees are mature, they create a gloomy, half-lit world beneath their canopy. The dark, endless sameness is broken only by mud strips that pass for roads for moving workers and rubber sap in and out. Monsoon season had turned the ruts into rivers of mud that in places could swallow a truck whole. Thankfully, JD has twenty years of experience with mud and got us through!

At the end of the road we reached Som Rah—a huddle of huts on the ragged fringe of the jungle. We gathered in a Krung house marked with a red cross nailed to the front of it. That little hut was a "Holy of Holies," for there we worshiped Jesus with voices and hands and instruments, including a drum covered with python skin. The believers sang of new life through Christ and praised him for setting them free from the slavery of sin and the service of demons. The Krung word for "hallelujah" is *Kī yo*, and their songs were accented with "Kī yo! Kī yo!" Many testimonies and words of encouragement were shared, too, including JD's recounting of our trip into Laos. JD challenged them: "You have the Bible, and you have the Holy Spirit. That is all you need to start churches and take the gospel to your people across the border in Laos."

As Pastor Naay preached the Word, it was beautiful to see the first generation of Krung Christians reading the Bible in their language. Afterwards, two deaconesses prepared the Lord's Table and distributed reminders of his sacrifice, and we sang a song of the cross. Not long ago these people were swallowed up with fear, slaves to the service of Satan; but the King has set them free and adopted them as his own! As we shared the Lord's Table as a family, I recalled the Scripture where it says,

"Once you were not a people, but now you are God's people; once you had not received mercy, but now you have received mercy" (1 Pet. 2:10).

Christians gather for worship in Som Rah village

There at the end of the road we worshiped—in awe of our Captain's brilliance and grace, amazed at his every-tribe-every-tongue gospel, and singing a song JD taught me long ago:

> I want to know Christ and the power of His rising,
> Share in His sacrifice, conform to His death.
> As I pour out my life to be filled with His Spirit,
> Joy follows suffering, and life follows death.[8]

# Epilogue

"And those who are wise shall shine like the brightness of the sky above; and those who turn many to righteousness, like the stars forever and ever."

*Daniel 12:3*

## Artillery Road
### *March 20, 2018*

This is the first day my schedule and the weather have allowed me to write on the back porch again. It's one of my favorite places. Murphy the Cat keeps me company, soaking up the sun and peering through the screen at the birdfeeders, which right now resemble the airspace over O'Hare. Cardinals, chickadees, nuthatches, goldfinches, grackles, jays, and juncos chatter and flutter in a swirl of color and song. It sounds like spring. It feels like home.

It's been a month in motion on three continents, but now it's time to stop and put the finishing touches on this book. The traveler Paul Theroux wrote, "You go away for a long time and return a different person—you never come all the way back."[1] After a lifetime of journeys, I understand this in a way that is not easy to put into words. What I have seen ranges from beautiful beyond description to ugly evil beyond forgetting.

However, the most important way all these journeys have changed me is in how my view of God has changed—or, better said, how he has been magnified before my eyes and in my heart. He is so much bigger, his gospel is so much more powerful, and his church so much more precious than I ever imagined!

When I was growing up, the race to send astronauts to the moon was in full swing. I would watch on television or listen by radio to get all the latest news about a rocket launch or lunar landing, even in the middle of the night. I read everything I could find on astronomy and rocketry and even built an experimental rocket that was a fiery failure! Above all, I dreamed of having a *real* telescope, but I didn't have the least hope of owning one. The price in the Sears Roebuck catalog made that clear. I knew there weren't enough lawns to cut for enough summers ahead to ever buy it. Then one Christmas morning, there it was. To this day, I get choked up thinking of how much my father and mother sacrificed in order to buy it for me. Christmases will always be crowned with memories of their extravagant love. It was a gift that would open up the heavens to me like my dad's binoculars never could.

My journeys (and the journals that have followed) have magnified God in much the same way to me. Every time I go to another corner of the world and see the church growing and the gospel changing lives, my view of God gets bigger. The men and women in this book are my heroes for the ways they magnify the grace and power of our risen Christ. Like stars in the heavens, they shine with glory that has been given to them by their Savior.

But there are many more stars out there, for we have a great King who is mighty to save. I want to get a closer look at as many as I can for as long as I can until I see the Maker of those stars for myself. I just read a report from a friend serving in Central Asia, where an Al-Qaeda affiliate is trying in vain to keep control. He wrote:

> Some Muslim radicals started putting pressure on our brothers. A mullah visited our brothers in Berezovka and

demanded that they deny Christ, and gave them three days to make that decision. Our brothers said they did not have to wait three days because they had already made a firm decision to follow Christ and weren't going to deny him. They answered in love and meekness but very firmly.

It's a pleasant morning here, but I want to go meet the brothers of Berezovka. It sounds like they bear a strong likeness to our King—and they have stories to tell.

# Notes

## Introduction

1. Stephen E. Ambrose, *Band of Brothers: E Company, 506th Regiment, 101st Airborne from Normandy to Hitler's Eagle's Nest* (New York: Simon & Schuster, 1992), 307.
2. Information recorded in the introduction to *Dispatches from the Front: A Bold Advance* (Frontline Missions International: 2010), DVD.
3. Charles Wesley, "O for a Thousand Tongues to Sing," 1740.
4. Justin Taylor, "Why and How John Piper Does Biography," *Evangelical History* (blog), May 24, 2017, https://blogs.thegospelcoalition.org /evangelical-history/2017/05/24/why-and-how-john-piper-does -biography/.
5. David McCullough, "David McCullough, The Art of Biography No. 2," interview by Elizabeth Gaffney and Benjamin Ryder Howe, *The Paris Review*, no. 152 (Fall 1999), https://www.theparisreview.org/interviews /894/david-mccullough-the-art-of-biography-no-2-david-mccullough.
6. Ambrose, *Band of Brothers*, 13.

## Chapter 1: Facing Fear

1. John Piper, *Filling Up the Afflictions of Christ: The Cost of Bringing the Gospel to the Nations in the Lives of William Tyndale, Adoniram Judson, and John Paton* (Wheaton, IL: Crossway, 2009), 26.
2. F. F. Bruce, *The Dawn of Christianity* (Grand Rapids, MI: Eerdmans, 1954), 168.
3. F. F. Bruce, *The Growing Day* (Grand Rapids, MI: Eerdmans, 1954), 36.
4. For more information see House Committee on Homeland Security, "Terrorism in North Africa: An Examination of the Threat," Testimony of Laith Alkhouri, March 29, 2017, http://docs.house.gov/meetings/HM/HM05 /20170329/105759/HHRG-115-HM05-Wstate-AlkhouriL-20170329.pdf.
5. See my "Awakening Today," *Tabletalk Magazine*, February 1, 2016, https:// www.ligonier.org/learn/articles/awakening-today/.
6. From *Dispatches from the Front: Day of Battle* (Frontline Missions International: 2014), DVD.

7. See my "Headscarves and Hashtags," desiringGod.org, March 8, 2016, https://www.desiringgod.org/articles/headscarves-and-hashtags/.

8. Ernie Pyle, *Brave Men* (New York: Grosset & Dunlap, 1944), 44.

9. Benoit Faucon and David Gauthier-Villars, "Attacks Put New Focus on Europe's Moroccan Diaspora," *The Wall Street Journal*, August 21, 2017, A7.

10. Charles Spurgeon, *Metropolitan Tabernacle Pulpit: Volume 30, 1884* (Pasadena, TX: Pilgrim Publications, 1986), 130.

11. Elisabeth Elliot, *These Strange Ashes* (Grand Rapids, MI: Revell, 1998), 145.

12. Ten days into their journey, Cesar and Joel were arrested for their gospel work. During the police interrogation, they were asked, "Who sent you here?" They replied, "Jesus Christ." "Why have you come?" They opened up one of their New Testaments and said, "It is right here." Then they read Matthew 28:19–21 and Acts 1:8. The officers, who had never seen a Bible before, carefully copied out these verses of Scripture into the police report. These two brothers also had a copy of a gospel film. Since this was "evidence" against these men, the entire police department watched the film! After being held three days, they appeared before a judge. God gave them wisdom and grace to answer him according to the Scripture. They were threatened—and then released. By God's grace, Cesar and Joel continued to share the gospel and respond to Bible requesters for another four months, until they were arrested again and deported. They returned to Peru and trained their replacements.

13. David Nichols, ed., *Ernie's War: The Best of Ernie Pyle's World War II Dispatches* (New York: Random House, 1986), 113.

*Chapter 2: The Glory of the Cross*

1. D. A. Carson, *Scandalous: The Cross and Resurrection of Jesus* (Wheaton, IL: Crossway, 2010), 103.

2. Samuel M. Zwemer, *Islam and the Cross* (Phillipsburg, NJ: P&R, 2002), 53.

3. Charles Spurgeon, *Metropolitan Tabernacle Pulpit, Volume 20, 1874* (Pasadena, TX: Pilgrim Publications, 1986), 223.

4. John R. W. Stott, *The Cross of Christ* (Downers Grove, IL: InterVarsity Press, 1986), 25, 40.

5. Samuel Zwemer, *The Glory of the Cross* (London: Marshall, Morgan & Scott, 1928), 6.

6. Samuel Zwemer, "The Cross in Christ's Commission," address at Urbana 46, December 1946, http://www.urbana.org/articles/the-cross-in-christs-commission-1946, accessed July 20, 2010.

7. Alfred DeWitt Mason and Frederick J. Barny, *History of the Arabian Mission* (New York: Board of Foreign Missions Reformed Church in America, 1926), 67.

8. Samuel M. Zwemer and James Cantine, *The Golden Milestone: Reminiscences of Pioneer Days Fifty Years Ago in Arabia* (London: Fleming H. Revell, 1938), 116.

9. Zwemer, *Islam and the Cross*, xvii.

10. Alexander Whyte, *Lancelot Andrewes and His Private Devotions* (1896; London: Kessinger Publishing, 2006), 114–15.

11. Caroline Cobb, "Wake Up" from *The Blood + The Breath: Songs That Sing the Story of Redemption*, www.carolinecobb.com. Used by permission.

*Chapter 3: The Character for Bravery*

1. C. S. Lewis, *The Voyage of the Dawn Treader*, The Chronicles of Narnia (1952; New York: HarperCollins, 2000), 187.

2. John Lyons and Yifan Xie, "Karmic Battle Takes Place on Shanghai River," *The Wall Street Journal*, May 30, 2017, A10.

3. Paul Theroux, *Ghost Train to the Eastern Star* (Boston: Houghton Mifflin, 2008), 90.

4. A. J. Broomhall, *Hudson Taylor and China's Open Century*, book 5, *Refiner's Fire* (London: Hodder and Stoughton and Overseas Missionary Fellowship, 1985), 350.

*Chapter 4: Mercy Multiplied.*

1. Thomas Fuller, *Truth Maintained* (Oxford: 1643), n.p. Quote is cited in Harry Christopher Minchin," Glimpses of Dr. Thomas Fuller," *The Fortnightly Review* (London: Chapman and Hall, 1908), 90:53.

*Chapter 5: A Hero in the Battle of Life*

1. Charles Haddon Spurgeon, *Morning and Evening Daily Readings* (Grand Rapids, MI: Zondervan, 1973), 262.

2. John Bunyan, *The Pilgrim's Progress* (1678; Edinburgh: Banner of Truth, 1979), 376.

*Chapter 6: Rise and Fight Again*

1. A. J. Broomhall, *Hudson Taylor and China's Open Century*, book 5, *Refiner's Fire* (London: Hodder and Stoughton and Overseas Missionary Fellowship, 1985), 78.

2. Richard M. Ketchum, ed., *The American Heritage Book of the Revolution* (New York: American Heritage, 1958), 209.

3. Ketchum, *American Heritage Book of the Revolution*, 321.

*Chapter 7: Shepherds*

1. John Bunyan, *The Pilgrim's Progress* (1678; Edinburgh: Banner of Truth, 1979), 257.

2. Ballington Booth, "The Cross Is Not Greater," 1892.

3. Bunyan, *The Pilgrim's Progress*, 376.

4. "The Look" Original words by John Newton (1725–1807), music and add. words by Bob Kauflin. © 2001 Sovereign Grace Praise (BMI). Sovereign Grace Music, a division of Sovereign Grace Churches. All rights reserved. Administrated worldwide at www.CapitolCMGPublishing.com, excluding the UK which is adm. by Integrity Music, part of the David C. Cook family. www.SovereignGraceMusic.org.

5. To learn more about the Joshua Project, visit www.joshuaproject.net.
6. Samuel M. Zwemer, *Islam and the Cross* (Phillipsburg, NJ: P&R, 2002), 26–27.
7. "All Creatures of Our God and King" Original words (vv. 1-2) by St. Francis of Assisi, translated by William Henry Draper. Music, 16th Century German tune, adapted by Jonathan Baird and Ryan Baird. Add. words (vv. 3-4) by Jonathan Baird and Ryan Baird. © 2013 Sovereign Grace Worship (ASCAP). Sovereign Grace Music, a division of Sovereign Grace Churches. All rights reserved. Administrated worldwide at www.Capitol CMGPublishing.com, excluding the UK which is adm. by Integrity Music, part of the David C. Cook family. www.SovereignGraceMusic.org.
8. Personal letter to Tim Keesee.
9. Martin Luther, "A Mighty Fortress Is Our God," 1529.
10. John Piper, "How the Supremacy of Christ Creates Radical Christian Sacrifice," sermon preached at Together for the Gospel conference, Louisville, KY, April 27, 2008, https://www.desiringgod.org/messages/how-the-supremacy-of-christ-creates-radical-christian-sacrifice.
11. Roger Steer, *J. Hudson Taylor: A Man in Christ* (Wheaton, IL: Harold Shaw, 1993), 173.

Chapter 8: Torn Curtain

1. Gordon Taylor, *Fever & Thirst: An American Doctor among the Tribes of Kurdistan, 1935–1844* (Chicago: Academy Chicago Publishers, 2005), 214.
2. David Satter, "100 Years of Communism—and 100 Million Dead," *The Wall Street Journal*, November 7, 2017, A17.
3. Satter, "100 Years of Communism," A17.
4. William Manchester and Paul Reid, *The Last Lion* (New York: Little, Brown and Company, 2012), 960.
5. Manchester and Reid, *The Last Lion*, 960.
6. Helen and Lewis Melville, *London's Lure: An Anthology in Prose & Verse* (London: George Bell & Sons, 1909), 215.
7. Dr. and Mrs. Howard Taylor, *Hudson Taylor and the China Inland Mission: The Growth of a Work of God* (OMF International, 1998), 279.
8. Isaac Watts, "When I Survey the Wondrous Cross," 1707.

Chapter 9: White Rose

1. John Piper, *A Sweet and Bitter Providence: Sex, Race, and the Sovereignty of God* (Wheaton, IL: Crossway, 2010), 121.
2. Often attributed to Adolphe-Louis-Frédéric-Théodore Monod (1802–1856).
3. Charles B. Wycuff, "I See Jesus," Lovely Name Music, 1957. Used by permission.

Chapter 10: Cell 44

1. Georgi Vins, *Testament from Prison* (Elgin, IL: David C. Cook, 1975), 62.

2. John Piper, "God Is Always Doing 10,000 Things in Your Life," desiringGod.org, January 1, 2013, https://www.desiringgod.org/articles/god-is-always-doing-10000-things-in-your-life.

3. Georgi Vins, *Gospel in Bonds* (Elkhart, IN: Russian Gospel Ministries, 1995), 87–88.

4. Jimmy Carter, *Keeping Faith: Memoirs of a President* (New York: Bantam, 1982), 147.

5. Vins, *Gospel in Bonds*, 88–90.

6. Carter, *Keeping Faith*, 147.

7. Vins, *Gospel in Bonds*, 90–91.

8. Carter, *Keeping Faith*, 147–49.

9. Vins, *Gospel in Bonds*, 91–92.

10. Carter, *Keeping Faith*, 149.

11. Letter to Tim Keesee, originally published in "A Year of Jubilee," *The Messenger*, Frontline Missions International (Fall 2004), 6–7.

12. Georgi Vins, "Cell 44," *Prisoner Bulletin*, 5, no. 1 (Spring 1984), 12.

Chapter 11: Martyrdom of Faithful

1. Edith Searell in Marshall Broomhall, ed., *Martyred Missionaries of the China Inland Mission with a Record of the Perils and Sufferings of Some Who Escaped* (Toronto: China Inland Mission, 1901), 29.

2. John Bunyan, *The Pilgrim's Progress* (1678; Edinburgh: Banner of Truth, 1979), 96.

3. Bunyan, *Pilgrim's Progress*, 109.

4. Bunyan, *Pilgrim's Progress*, 110.

5. W. P. Livingstone, *Mary Slessor of Calabar: Pioneer Missionary* (London: Hodder and Stoughton, 1916), 324.

6. Thomas Watson in I. D. E. Thomas, ed., *A Puritan Golden Treasury* (Carlyle, PA: Banner of Truth, 2000), 246.

7. The exponential increase in the number of suicide bombers is just one aspect of Islam's deep darkness. In the 1980s, the global average of suicide bombings was three a year. In the 1990s, it was one a month. In the early 2000s, there was one a week, and by 2015 one a day. While Islamists call suicide bombers "martyrs," they really are just mass murderers who kill and maim thousands of innocent people each year. For more information see "Chicago Project on Security and Terrorism. Suicide Attack Database," http://cpostdata.uchicago.edu/search_new.php.

8. Robert D. Kaplan, *Soldiers of God: With the Mujahidin in Afghanistan* (Houghton Mifflin: Boston, 1990), 49.

9. Timothy Keller, *Walking with God through Pain and Suffering* (New York: Viking, 2013), 59.

10. Karen Money, "Surrender," from *Secret Things* (September 2005). Used by permission.

11. John Kent, "Sovereign Grace O'er Sin Abounding," *A New Selection of Seven Hundred Evangelical Hymns*, ed. John Dobell (Morristown, NJ: Peter A. Johnson, 1810), 634.
12. Samuel M. Zwemer and Amy E. Zwemer, *Topsy-Turvy Land: Arabia Pictured for Children* (New York: Revell, 1902), 116.
13. Ballington Booth, "The Cross Is Not Greater," 1892.
14. Cheryl Beckett song based on Isaiah 43, from an email to the author from Beth Kaessner, September 4, 2010. Used by permission.

*Chapter 12: Incurable Optimism*
1. Mark Wise, in personal letter to Tim Keesee.
2. "Unclassified Version of Director of Central Intelligence George J. Tenet's Testimony before the Joint Inquiry into Terrorist Attacks against the United States," CIA website, June 18, 2002. https://www.cia.gov/news-information/speeches-testimony/2002/dci_testimony_06182002.html.
3. Dave Furman, "No Greater Gospel: An Interview with Dave Furman," Ligonier.org, from *Tabletalk Magazine*, July 1, 2014, https://www.ligonier.org/learn/articles/no-greater-gospel/.
4. "How Firm a Foundation," 1787.
5. Samuel M. Zwemer, *The Unoccupied Mission Fields of Africa and Asia* (New York: Student Volunteer Movement for Foreign Missions, 1911), 226.
6. Samuel M. Zwemer, *Islam and the Cross* (Phillipsburg, NJ: P&R, 2002), 144.
7. George Herbert in *The Complete English Works* (New York: Alfred A. Knopf, 1995), 39.
8. Charles Wesley, "Christ the Lord Is Risen Today," 1739.

*Chapter 13: "He Showed Them His Hands"*
1. Samuel Zwemer, "The Cross in Christ's Commission," address at Urbana 46, December 1946, http://www.urbana.org/articles/the-cross-in-christs-commission-1946, accessed July 20, 2010.
2. "Out of the Depths" Music and words by Bob Kauflin. © 2008 Sovereign Grace Praise (BMI). Sovereign Grace Music, a division of Sovereign Grace Churches. All rights reserved. Administrated worldwide at www.CapitolCMGPublishing.com, excluding the UK which is adm. by Integrity Music, part of the David C. Cook family. www.SovereignGraceMusic.org.
3. Timothy Keller, *King's Cross: The Story of the World in the Life of Jesus* (New York: Penguin, 2011), 224.
4. Abraham Kuyper, inaugural lecture at the Free University of Amsterdam, October 20, 1880, quoted in *Abraham Kuyper: A Centennial Reader*, ed. James D. Bratt (Grand Rapids, MI: Eerdmans, 1998), 488.
5. Janine di Giovanni, *The Morning They Came for Us: Dispatches from Syria* (New York: Liveright, 2016), 123–24.

*Chapter 14: Things as They Are*

1. A. J. Broomhall, *Hudson Taylor and China's Open Century*, book 5, *Refiner's Fire* (London: Hodder and Stoughton and Overseas Missionary Fellowship, 1985), 350.
2. Amy Wilson-Carmichael, *Things As They Are: Mission Work in Southern India* (London: Morgan and Scott, 1903), 188.
3. Elisabeth Elliot, *A Chance to Die: The Life and Legacy of Amy Carmichael* (Grand Rapids, MI: Fleming H. Revell, 1987), 171.
4. Wilson-Carmichael, *Things As They Are*, 41–44.
5. Wilson-Carmichael, *Things As They Are*, 158.
6. Wilson-Carmichael, *Things As They Are*, 158–59.
7. Shared in a personal letter from a missionary friend to Tim Keesee.
8. Elliot, *A Chance to Die*, 176–78.
9. Mary Drewery, *William Carey: A Biography* (Grand Rapids, MI: Zondervan, 1979), 39.
10. John Piper, *Andrew Fuller: Holy Faith, Worthy Gospel, World Mission* (Wheaton, IL: Crossway, 2016), 13.
11. Terry G. Carter, ed., *The Journal and Selected Letters of William Carey* (Macon, GA: Smyth & Helwys, 1999), 51–52.
12. Tim Challies, "The History of Christianity in 25 Objects: William Carey's Couch," *Challies* (blog), February 6, 2014, https://www.challies.com/articles/the-history-of-christianity-in-25-objects-william-careys-couch/.
13. Mark Twain, *Following the Equator: A Journey around the World* (New York: Harper & Brothers, 1897), 300.

*Chapter 15: The Broken Sword*

1. William Cowper, "God Moves in a Mysterious Way," 1774.
2. See my article "Opportunity," Frontline International website, July 25, 2014, https://www.frontlinemissions.info/news/1887.
3. Edward Sills, "Opportunity," in William J. Bennett, ed., *The Moral Compass: Stories for a Life's Journey* (New York: Simon & Schuster, 1995), 268.
4. Transcribed from the Q&A closing session at the Frontline Experience Conference hosted by Frontline Missions International at Bethlehem Baptist Church, Minneapolis, MN, October 13–15, 2016.

*Chapter 16: Aslan Is on the Move*

1. Paul Theroux, *The Happy Isles of Oceania: Paddling the Pacific* (New York: G.P. Putnam's Sons, 1992), 446.
2. William Blake, "Preface to Milton: A Poem in Two Books," in *The Complete Poetry and Prose of William Blake*, ed. David V. Erdman (New York: Anchor, 1988), 95.
3. C. S. Lewis, *The Lion, the Witch and the Wardrobe* (1950; New York: Harper Collins, 2000), 79.
4. C. S. Lewis, *Surprised by Joy* (1955; San Francisco: HarperOne, 2017), 234.

5. C. S. Lewis, *Mere Christianity* (1952; San Francisco: HarperCollins, 2001), 136–37.
6. C. S. Lewis, *The Weight of Glory* (1949; New York: HarperOne, 2009), 26.
7. Carolyn Weber, *Surprised by Oxford: A Memoir* (Nashville: W Publishing Group, 2011), 327.
8. Vaughan Roberts, "Stay Free!" sermon at St. Ebbe's Church, Oxford, England, February 11, 2018.
9. Krissy Nordhoff, Michael Farren, Riley Engquist, "Oh Praise (The Only One)" Copyright © 2015 Centricity Music Publishing (ASCAP) Farren Love and War Pub (SESAC) Integrity's Alleluia! Music (SESAC) (adm. At CapitolCMGPublishing.com) Used by permission.
10. Nordhoff, Farren, and Engquist, "Oh Praise (The Only One)."

*Chapter 17: End of the Road*

1. Samuel Zwemer, *Call to Prayer* (London: Marshall Brothers, n.d.), 68.
2. Alan Seeger, "I Have a Rendezvous with Death," in *One Hundred and One Famous Poems*, ed. Roy J. Cook (Chicago: The Cable Company, 1929), 10.
3. Philip Short, *Pol Pot: Anatomy of a Nightmare* (New York: Henry Holt, 2004), 10–11.
4. Short, *Pol Pot*, 12–13.
5. John Piper, "I Am Sending You Out as Sheep in the Midst of Wolves," desiringGod.org, October 21, 2007, https://www.desiringgod.org/messages /i-am-sending-you-out-as-sheep-in-the-midst-of-wolves#full-audio, 9:38–ff.
6. Andrew Peterson, "Hosanna," *Resurrection Letters Vol II* (Centricity Music, 2008). Used by permission.
7. Bart D. Ehrman, *Forged: Writing in the Name of God—Why the Bible's Authors Are Not Who We Think They Are* (New York: Harper Collins, 2011), 74–75.
8. Anonymous, "The Power of His Rising" (harmonization copyright, Fred and Ruth Coleman, 2013). Used by permission.

*Epilogue*

1. Paul Theroux, *Dark Star Safari: Overland from Cairo to Cape Town* (New York: Houghton Mifflin, 2002), 470.

# Dispatches from the Front DVD Series

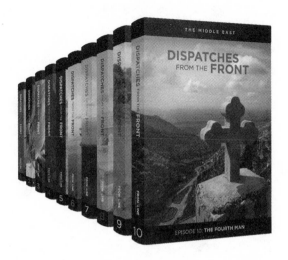

Each episode in this DVD series follows the stories of God's work in the distant corners of the earth, opening our eyes to the advance of Christ's kingdom all over the world. The writing and filming unfold in each moment, with no scripting or staging. The sights and sounds of daily activity on the front lines will serve to unite our hearts with our brothers and sisters in different parts of the world, awaken us out of our comfortable Christianity, and expand our vision of the King and his powerful gospel.

"The narrative is as beautifully crafted
as the stories are inspiring."

**JOHN PIPER,** Founder, desiringGod.org

"This series of presentations gives us a non-hyped view of amazing faithfulnesses—amazing faithfulness of cross-cultural Christian workers, of pastors, and, most of all, of God. They are exciting, humbling, faith building, and prayer encouraging."

**MARK DEVER,** Pastor, Capitol Hill Baptist Church

---

To place an order or view trailers and video clips,
visit **dispatchesfromthefront.org**.

New *Dispatches from the Front* episodes coming Summer 2019.

# Also Available from Tim Keesee

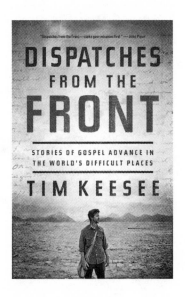

"*Dispatches from the Front* is a thoughtful, moving, understated, and ultimately convicting narrative depicting the work of the gospel in some of the most challenging corners of the world. To read of the kingdom advance in the teeth of challenges is to learn humility and rekindle contrition, faith, and intercessory prayer."

**D. A. CARSON,** Research Professor of New Testament, Trinity Evangelical Divinity School; Cofounder, The Gospel Coalition

"Tim Keesee has a remarkable ministry in traveling the world to seek out what the Lord is doing and to make these things known. *Dispatches from the Front* allows you to travel with him, and if you go along, you will be blessed, you will be encouraged, and you will praise God."

**TIM CHALLIES,** blogger, *Challies.com*

For more information, visit **crossway.org**.